THE

SOUND

OF THE

SPIRIT

UNLOCKING THE MYSTERIES OF PRAISE AND WORSHIP

DR. HARRY SALEM III

Unlocking the Mysteries of Praise and Worship
ISBN 1-890370-28-2

Copyright © 2015 by Salem Family Ministries

Fourth Printing

Salem Family Ministries
PO Box 1595
Cathedral City, CA 92345
www.salemfamilyministries.org

Disclaimer: The views expressed in this workbook contain my personal opinions and experiences throughout my life and time spent in God's presence. I express them as my opinion and view only, and share them with you from my personal lifelong experience from my heart. I am only communicating what has worked for me personally, and what I have personally experienced with the Lord.

Chapter One

Lucifer, the Blessed and the Outcast

When dealing with praise and worship to Jehovah God, it is important to understand their origins. Though all things originate from God, it is understandable that it is God's creations that are the administrators and instruments of all that He creates. In terms of praise, worship, music, and beauty, the first to be set over these things was the angel Lucifer.

Although the biography of Lucifer is not exactly known, save for what is said in the Bible, there is one thing that is known about Lucifer that can't be argued. Out of all the angels in heaven, he was the most adorned, and the most highly decorated angel in all of the kingdom of God. Lucifer was not only an alleged archangel (which supposedly consisted of himself, Michael, and Gabriel), but also was of the cherubim order of angels.

There are many classifications of angels in the heavenly realm. The highest order would be those of the seraphim. These are the angels who guard and care for the throne room of God. Described in Isaiah 6:2, seraphim have six wings. Two covering their faces, two covering their feet, and two used to fly. In Revelations 4:8 they are described as the four living creatures with eyes all around and within them. They are constantly saying, *"Holy, holy, holy is the Lord God Almighty, who was and is and is to come!"* Following the seraphim, the cherubim are the second highest rank and class of the nine fold celestial hierarchy of angels.

Like the seraphim, the cherubim are depicted as creature like angels. Ezekiel 10:13-22 gives detailed information on the cherubim's physical descriptions such as they have four faces of a cherub (ox, angel), a human, a lion, and an eagle. Some translations of the Bible use the word ox instead of angel, and other translations use the word angel. In the ancient Hebrew language this particular face represents the strength of the creatures. It is derived from the first letter of the ancient Hebrew alphabet which is the face of an ox and means 'strong.' They have eyes covering their entire bodies including their wings. In Middle Eastern art, the cherubim are often represented as a lion or a bull with eagle's wings. In Jewish tradition the lion and the bull are both symbols of Jewish royalty. The word cherubim or cherub is a Hebrew word that's roots are taken from a Babylonian word 'karabu.' This word is translated into meaning great or mighty.

In Isaiah 14:12, there is a description of Lucifer in regards to his fall from heaven. The verse states, *"How you have fallen from heaven morning star, son of the dawn! You have been cast down to the earth, you who once laid low the nations!"* The interesting parts to this scripture are the titles that Isaiah uses when describing Lucifer. Such names as 'morning star' and 'son of the dawn' are used. While these titles are used in a scripture that describe Lucifer's condemnation, it is important to point out that these very well could have been the titles of adornment during his time in the service to God. Indeed, Lucifer was the most glorious of all the angels set apart in heaven. He was the angel of music and beauty, a commander of a third of the angelic forces of heaven, and the chief worshiper of the Most High God.

It can be understood how a person's ego could get too high and mighty from a position of such power and authority. Besides this, however, it can be agreed that Lucifer was a very important person in the heavenly host. It can be surmised that he was an artist and musician as well due to his duties as chief of worship and music.

Imagine being in his position for a moment if you will. Before the universe was filled with sin, before the great wars that would be fought between good and evil, and even before death existed there was only this perfect time when anything and everything could happen. Imagine being the prince of music, the composer for the glorious sounds that would resonate throughout the heavens. Imagine being the architect of the melodies and symphonies that would give glory and honor to the Lord of hosts. Having the ability to use beauty as you see fit, to use color, light, sound, and any and all things to make the most radiant and amazing sounds that would never be duplicated or recaptured save only for the most blessed of imaginations. This is what Lucifer was, the angel of music; a bright and shining star.

In I John 1:5, it says that, *"God is light and no darkness comes from Him."* This is a statement not only of God, but of His place of dwelling as well. Due to this account from John, it is best to assume that all who were in the heavenly realm were beings of light. Lucifer then would best be described as the brightest of all the angels.

In Luke 10:18, Luke is giving an account of seeing Satan fall from heaven like a bolt of lightning. In another translation of this scripture, it states that Luke saw a bright shining star falling from the heavens to earth. Though the Bible does have many translations, it is agreeable that what was seen of Satan in his descent towards earth was a bright and shining being of light.

While his descent from heaven is important, it is not the issue for the moment. The issue is Lucifer and his role while he was still the angel of music. This angel had command of all things music, light, beauty, and he was the best at what he did. It would be interesting to hear some of the melodies that he created for the worship of the Most High God, if it were possible to hear them.

At the time before the story of creation in the book of Genesis, it was Lucifer who was anointed with the gifts of praise and worship. He was "the angel" in charge of all things beauty and music. These kinds of esteemed positions often can produce negative emotions, and that could often lead to very dangerous points of thought.

The book of Ezekiel contains scriptures on ′ Lucifer was in his time as an angel of God. They give a description of him as a being of wisdom, unblemished beauty, and an anointed cherub. That all changed when, according to Ezekiel 28:14,15, and 17, he allowed his heart to become proud, having unrighteousness find him and his wisdom then becoming corrupted. It further reads that at one time Lucifer spent time on God's holy mountain, and could walk through the midst of stones of fire.

The name Lucifer is the English translation of the Latin Vulgate word that means morning star, or light bringing. The name of Lucifer in Hebrew is Helel which is mentioned only once in the Hebrew Bible. The Greek name of Lucifer, Heosphoros, is also a representation of morning star as Heosphoros translates to bringer of the dawn.

It is without much doubt that Lucifer was perhaps the greatest of the angels of heaven, or at least one of the more prominent ones. If we take the scripture of Ezekiel 28:14 and look at it from a viewing of placement, we can assume that Lucifer spent his days in the very presence of God Himself. The idea of the holy mountain can be assumed to be God's dwelling place. Like the scripture says in regards to walking through stones of fire, Lucifer was able to do things that no one else could. From all of this, the question that must be asked is what would cause Lucifer, the anointed cherub and archangel, to rebel against God and become Satan, the adversary to God?

We read in scripture that Lucifer rebelled and waged war against God in the hopes of taking His throne and establishing himself above the stars of God. In Isaiah 14:12-15, Isaiah goes into detail on a proclamation that Lucifer said about ascending to heaven above the stars of God, and sitting on the mount of assembly. Lucifer was proclaiming his ascendancy to an authority title above God Himself. What is to be studied here is not that Lucifer was attempting to take over the throne of God, but why was he trying to take over God's kingdom?

Let's look at something for a moment about the mind and logic. In Romans 8:27-28, the Apostle Paul writes, *"Now He who searches the hearts knows what the mind of the spirit is, because He makes intercessions for the saints according to the will of God. And we know that all things work together for good to those who love God, to those who are called according to His purpose."* This scripture, while describing Jesus, has the point to be made for showing "Those who know the mind of the spirit."

Now, we know that Lucifer spent time in the very presence of God. He was the administrator of worship and chief musician. He was an anointed cherub, an archangel, and a warrior who commanded a 3rd of the forces of heaven. Apart from these titles, he was in the very midst of the spirit daily with God. As humans who are created in the image of God, we must strive daily to understand the knowledge of God, His lessons, and His spirit. Before man existed though there was this angel.

Is it not agreeable to say that Lucifer was aware of the very knowledge of God, the word of God; the Word that is, was, and is to come? If Lucifer was aware of the plan of each and everyone's purpose, each ones individual and unique life in God, and God's own uniqueness among

His creations, is it possible that Lucifer realized he could never be God?

The Bible does not say that he was unaware of the power of God, nor does it say that he was not knowledgeable on the very nature, power, or word of God. Isaiah stated that he wanted to ascend above God, but it is very possible that Lucifer knew that he could never be the One who created him. Though angels are not human, they are sentient beings that are given purposes, gifts, and free will that make them unique in the service of God. Lucifer, being of the status that he was in, was constantly rising higher and higher in everything he did. Like God, he was a creator, being able to create magnificent sounds, songs, works of beauty, and so much more. But, the one thing that separated Lucifer from God was the simple fact that it was God who created Lucifer, and not he who created God.

Lucifer came from the One who was there before anything was. God was the Word before the Word became form, and would be what all else came from today which we all know and call as life today. This meant that Lucifer's word would never be God's word, for it held no power as God's word did. Each word of God created a special and unique lesson, life, and meaning when spoken or heard. The unique word of God was the basis for the relationship between God and man, God and angel. It created the unique individual that was special between each and everyone that had relationship with the Father.

For Lucifer, this Word that would create uniqueness was something he could never have nor duplicate. It is in this logic and state of mind that we can assume was the moment when Lucifer gave into sin. Sin in itself is the very opposite nature of God. Let us presume in short order that everything of God is a constant positive. Therefore sin would be the exact opposite, a constant negative. In sin, there is no uniqueness and no individuality. Everything in sin is based on conformity to the nature of sin. Sin was before the fall of Lucifer, and sin will exist long after Lucifer takes his place in the Lake of Fire.

To point it out, sin did not originate with Lucifer. Lucifer was merely the first individual to sin, but sin itself was a force all its own. Angel and man can both operate in the nature of sin as it is a part of the very fabric of the universe, of the fabric of time and space. When man sinned, it created the same conformity that is shared with Lucifer and his angels. The point to this explanation of sin is that it was in this manner to which Lucifer chose to operate in once he decided to rebel against God.

For Lucifer to rebel against God, the acting on sin was to give him his own word. The word of the opposite too God, the word of the lie, the deception, and the truth to conformity is what Lucifer chose. Lucifer became the catalyst to what would become the word of sin, the word that would forever separate the special individual relationship from the One who is the Word. This Word that God is can also be called the Word of Life.

In Ezekiel 28:16, it states, *"In abundance of your trade you were filled with violence in your midst, and you sinned; so I cast you as a profane thing from the mountain of God, and I destroyed you, O guardian cherub, from the midst of the stones of fire."* God saw that Lucifer had chosen his own path which was filled with sin over God. Lucifer was cast out of the presence of God, off His holy mountain, and away from the protection and covering of the Almighty. Everything that was given to him, the gifts of the Spirit to praise and worship God, to create music and beauty, to be the most anointed in the presence of God was stripped from him by the Lord.

Now the Bible does not say that he was turned into some hideous form, some red horned monster, or some other type of depiction that is made by man. In II Corinthians 11:14 it says that, *"And no wonder, for even Satan himself disguises himself as an angel of light."* This disguise could still be his true form as the angel of beauty, but without the majesty of the covering of God. What is known outside of this scripture in II Corinthians on the physical appearance is that Lucifer was cast out of heaven like lightning, and his glory covering was removed from him and his angels.

In Ezekiel 28:15, we see Lucifer being described as blameless until unrighteousness was found in him. Like the spotless lamb that the Israelites would sacrifice before the altar to atone for sin to God, and like the perfect Lamb of God, Jesus, who bore our sins on the cross; Lucifer was at one time a blameless, sinless creature. After his fall, his covering was taken, his gifts removed, and his glory stripped from him. It states in Ezekiel 28:13, *"You were in Eden, the garden of God; every precious stone was your covering, sardius, topaz, and diamond, beryl, onyx, and jasper, sapphire, emerald, and carbuncle; and crafted in gold, were your settings and your engravings. On the day that you were created they were prepared."* Lucifer had everything a person could ever want, and yet it was not enough. He threw it all away because he simply could not be God, or God's word. On top of his fall, his angels who followed him also fell from the grace of God.

Matthew 25:41 states, *"Depart from me, you cursed, into the eternal fire prepared for the devil and his angels."* On the day of the fall, one-third of the angels of heaven fell with Lucifer. There was a great war in heaven between Satan and his angels against God and His angels. In Revelation 12:7-9 we see the verses describe a great war in heaven between the dragon who is Lucifer, and the archangel Michael, who commands the warring angels of heaven. Lucifer lost, of course, and in his loss came the fall of everyone with him to the earth.

In II Peter 2:4, we see God describing how the angels who had sinned were cast into hell, committed to chains of gloomy darkness, and were then sentenced to await their final judgment. This was the price of all according to Jude 1:6 who, *"did not stay within their position of their own authority, but left their proper dwelling,"* and sided with Lucifer against God.

What is unique about the fall of Lucifer to the earth is that once he fell, his gifts fell with him. It is interesting to note that when his gifts fell, they were taken from him and given to God's newest creation, humanity. Psalm 19:14 reads, *"Let the words of my mouth and the meditation of my heart be acceptable in Your sight, O Lord, my rock and my Redeemer."* (English Standard Version) When the gifts of praise and worship fell to the earth, they were given to the creation that God had called man.

His newest creation was made in the "image of God,"

and had the ability to create, to destroy, to speak things into existence, and to cast blessings and curses by the words of their mouths. As Psalm 19:14 mentioned above states, God is the rock and Redeemer to man. Interesting how the scriptures of Ezekiel speak about being able to walk on rocks of fire by having the protection of God, and then how the Psalm describes God as the rock and Redeemer to man.

When viewing both the Psalm and Ezekiel scriptures together perhaps the rocks of fire are God as the rock, the fire, and the protection all in one. The meaning simply is changed from one Biblical author, 40 authors of the Bible in total spanning 4,000 years respectively, to the next. They all have the same consistent message that God is the rock, the Redeemer, and the all-consuming fire.

The fire that is of God is a holy fire, but the words of the worshiper could very well be the protection against the fire's ability to burn. This could be seen and explained in two ways. The first is that as God, Jesus can enter into God, the Father's holy fire, because He is the holy fire. The second is that as God, the Son, Jesus, is the Word and therefore the holy fire is a part of Him as it is God, the Father, and therefore protected by the Word. Proverbs 10:11 states, *"The mouth of the righteous is a fountain of life."* Jesus is the way, the truth, and the life, and like water to fire in the physical, waters of life in the spirit can shield the same way from holy fire.

John 8:44 described Lucifer, who became Satan, the adversary to God after the fall, as having nothing to do with the truth because he has no truth in him. The definition of "the truth" would be Jesus, and this having no more of His truth in him would no longer give him the protection of living waters. It is for this that Satan no longer has access to God's rocks of fire, or Jesus' living water. His power of worship, the power and authority of his own words would now be removed from him. His word, the word of sin, would now be the only thing left for Satan to operate in, the only authority left for his angels to manifest. Now, his authority and power would be given to the very creation, humanity that was going to have to have Jesus die for their sins and save them. His gifts in creation of music, song, worship, praise, and even beauty would all be given to the human race.

In a way, it would be a precursor to what would happen to Israel's first king, Saul. He would choose his own path instead of God's, and after failing to atone would lose all his kingdom and authority to the second king of Israel, David.

The fall of Lucifer was the first act of sin ever to take place in existence. It could be argued that while the act of sin was bad, the real tragedy that transpired was when Lucifer thought in sin. In 1 Corinthians 8:2 it states, *"And if any man think that he knows anything, he knows nothing yet as he ought to know."* Further, in Philippians 4:8, the verse says, *"Whatever things are true, whatever things are pure...if there be any virtue, and if there be any praise, think on these things."* This should have been the mindset that Lucifer operated in on a constant whole.

As the chief worshiper, it was his responsibility to operate within the authority in the positions that he was appointed. When he thought on other things that were not of God, he had already committed sin in his heart.

This is not to say that angels, and human beings included, can't think on other things. The gift of free will gives each individual the right to think and decide on things of their own accord. As Philippians 4:8, and I Corinthians 8:2 states though, we must be careful what we think on. Thinking and dwelling on positive things, good things, and things of virtue can lead to a positive mindset that can foster great atmospheres of possibilities in people. But, if a person thinks on the wrong things, or assumes that they know everything, then they haven't learned anything. They instead think within the realms of ignorance and stupidity.

Satan allowed all the wrong things into his life and spirit when he became too prideful and full of himself. As we have learned, he began to operate on his own and not within the authority of God. His arrogance, pride, and desire to live by his own word set within him the spirit of rebellion and defiance. His anointing at this point was taken away from him. The anointing of God has the potential to come onto anyone, but it can be taken away just as easily if it is not used according to the authority God expects it to be used. What is also obvious about Lucifer was not only that his anointing was removed, but so was his covering of the Holy Spirit.

God operates within a trinity of three parts in Himself. This trinity is made up of God the Father, God the Son Jesus, and the Holy Spirit. All three operate as both one body, and then operate as One being in three bodies. Humanity operates with the Holy Spirit on earth. This was brought about due to the Holy Spirit coming to earth after Jesus ascended to heaven forty days after his resurrection. Of interest in regards to the operations of the Holy Spirit is that Jesus operated in the Holy Spirit while He was a man because He was no longer in His divine form.

Jesus, operating with the Holy Spirit, was an example of the future relationship between other human beings and the relationship with the Holy Spirit because Jesus was a human being while on the earth. The purpose of Jesus working with the Holy Spirit was to teach about the relationship that was given with Him that would establish a working of each person's authority according to his or her gifts in God. While an angel is not a human being, and has their own authority they operate in based on their position in God, they also operate and move based on certain flows of the Spirit.

On earth, or the earthly realm in another definition, angels of both light and dark can operate within the spirit. They fight and wage wars over the souls of man, but it is the flow of the spirit that determines how a battle is played out. In church praise and worship time, or in other kinds of Christian services, the flow of the spirit can determine whether or not how best angels can operate. In terms of worship to God, the Holy Spirit can manifest itself when the worship is true and at a certain level in the congregation or gathering of people. In Matthew 3:11 John the Baptist declared, *"I baptize you with water for repentance, but He who is coming after me is mightier than I, whose sandals I am not worthy to carry. He will baptize you with the Holy Spirit and fire."* The apostle Paul said in Romans 8:9, *"You, however, are not in the flesh but in the spirit, if in fact the spirit of God dwells in you. Anyone who does not have the spirit of Christ does not belong to Him."* Having the Holy Spirit in your life brings you a relationship with God that is unique and manifests the gifts He has given you in great abundance.

The manifesting of the Holy Spirit is the key to bring about the climate of a great movement of the spirit in praise and worship. While angels do operate in their own authority different than humans, those that operate in worship work in league with the Holy Spirit. With Lucifer, his whole existence and purpose would no doubt require a relationship with the Holy Spirit as he was a being of worship.

When Lucifer rebelled, the manifesting of the Holy Spirit was stripped from him. Not only did he lose his gifts and titles, but he had lost the relationship with God that set him and his gifts at the highest levels. Now, his gifts of worship and praise, his beauty, his light, and his creativity would be given to a majority, which would become man. Not only this, but now the Holy Spirit would operate with humanity as well, and set them on high in the kingdom of God. The Holy Spirit would give man the holy fire, the living waters, and the gift and interpretation of the tongues. Now they would walk in the Word, operate in the Word, manifest and create in the Word and strive in abundance with the Holy Spirit. As it says in Nehemiah 9:20, *"You gave your good spirit to instruct them, and did not withhold your manna from their mouth and gave them water for their thirst."* The Holy Spirit is the living water of God given to humanity.

Chapter Two

The Holy Spirit, God's Word and Voice on Earth

As human beings, do we understand the value of the Holy Spirit? Do we understand that this being that operates on earth is the same as Jesus the Son and God the Father? Do we respect Him and His role as helper to us on earth? These are questions that come to mind when thinking on the Holy Spirit. Another question that is sometimes asked is what is His role in matters of praise and worship?

The term Holy Spirit comes from the Hebrew name Ruach Hakodesh. This translates into Holy Spirit, or spirit of YHWH in the Hebrew Bible and other Jewish writings. Holy Spirit or Ruach Hakodesh is defined as divine aspect of wisdom and prophecy, divine force, and influence of the Most High God.

Let us take a look at His history and origins within the Bible. The first mentioning of the Holy Spirit starts in the New Testament with John the Baptist. There are mentions in the Old Testament about the spirit of God, but the name Holy Spirit is used in the New Testament. In Matthew 3:11, John declares," I baptize you with water for repentance, but He (Jesus) who is coming after me is mightier than I, whose sandals I am not worthy to carry. He will baptize you with the Holy Spirit and fire." John the Baptist, being the forerunner of Christ, was preparing the way for the arrival of Jesus and the Holy Spirit. Save for prophecy, it was not John's destiny to operate in the Holy Spirit's gifts as Christ would, but to prepare humanity to receive them. The true teachings and applications of the Holy Spirit would be revealed through Jesus Himself.

While John the Baptist is the teacher of the arrival of the Holy Spirit, Jesus would be the teacher of the applications of the Holy Spirit. As a man, Jesus no longer had His divine nature as God. Though He was still by definition God or the Son of God, His nature as a human was just that, as a human. It was in fact John who first empowered Jesus with the Holy Spirit after being tasked with the job of baptizing Him. It was at the instruction of Jesus that it had to be done in order for Him to receive the Holy Spirit. He was to set the example of how other people in the future would be baptized in the fire of God, and then receive the Holy Spirit. Luke 4:1 says after the baptism, "And Jesus, full of the Holy Spirit, returned from the Jordan and was led by the spirit in the wilderness."

When the Holy Spirit is allowed to come into existence in a person's life, the spirit will then begin to guide them in the ways that they should operate in their life. For

Jesus, operating in the spirit would be in the realm of teaching, ministry, and healing. Acts 10:38 says, *"How God anointed Jesus of Nazareth with the Holy Spirit and with power. He went about doing good and healing all who were oppressed by the devil, for God was with Him."*

The application of the Holy Spirit on earth is the application of God's power in the natural realm. The use of the Holy Spirit or Holy Ghost in the natural realm was to bring about the full potential of a human being in what they were originally created for. In I Corinthians 6:19 we read, *"Or do you not know that your body is a temple of the Holy Spirit within you, whom you have from God? You are not you own."* In Acts 1:8 we read, *"But you will receive power when the Holy Spirit has come upon you, . . ."* which was a testimony builder to the Apostle Paul and his helpers to be witnesses for God's gospel. The Holy Spirit is, in the simplest terms, a tool to evolve human beings past what they are in the physical world, which is covered in sin, to a higher state of what they were originally made for. That being the image of God able to perform and operate in the authority of their Creator to do the impossible!

Many people don't realize that as we are created in the image of God, so too do we have His power and abilities. While we are not God, we are able to do the things that He is capable of doing. This was the original purpose that God had planned for His creation when He first made man. In Exodus 35:31-35, we read a description of being filled with the spirit of God on certain sons of Israel as Moses spoke over them. It says starting in verse 31, *"And He had filled him with the spirit of God, in wisdom, in understanding, and in knowledge, and in all manners of workmanship; and to devise curious works, to work in gold, and in silver, and in brass. In the cutting of stones to set them, in carving of wood. and make any manner of cunning work. He had put in his heart that he may teach...them that he had filled with wisdom of heart, to work all manner of work, of the engraver, and of the cunning workman, and of the embroiderer, in blue, and in purple, in scarlet, and in fine linen, and of the weaver, even of them that do any work, and of those that devise cunning work."* Such a moving passage to use as an example when describing the abilities after being filled with the Holy Ghost!

Speaking with examples of the Holy Spirit from the Old Testament, referred to as the spirit of God, a perfect one concerning of the Holy Spirit applied to the gifts of praise and worship would be with King David. In the early days of Israel and its royal lineages, the first king of Israel, King Saul, had been at one time been filled with the spirit of God. When he rebelled against God, then the spirit of God had left him and had rested upon the shoulders of David while he was still a shepherd.

In I Samuel 16:14, we see a story about King Saul being tormented by an evil spirit. King Saul had sent away for David to come and play music for him in the hopes of granting him peace from the spirit. It is perhaps possible that Saul was under extreme duress and a spirit of depression and possibly suicide had rested on Saul due to the fact that he had earlier been told by Samuel that his kingdom was going to be given to another. Whatever the spirit on Saul, David came and played his music on the harp for him. The music worked, and in I Samuel 16:17 we see that whenever Saul was tormented, the songs of David would refresh Saul and give him peace.

This peace was brought about by the spirit of God that had rested on David. The songs that David would play and sing for Saul were actually songs of praise to God. When he would play his songs, the spirit would depart from Saul because the spirit of the Lord was resting over him. The movement of the Holy Spirit, when in league with worship, can create an atmosphere of healing and restoration. It is so powerful that no evil could ever come against it, and would have no power. It could be theorized that the anointing that David had was a precursor to the anointing and authority that Jesus would have on the earth years later as it would be David's lineage that Jesus would descend. This could make sense as David was described as a man after God's own heart, and it would be the blood of this man that God Himself would later come from when He became flesh and blood.

A 19th century essayist named Thomas Carlyle from Scotland once said that "Worship is transcendent wonder. Wonder for which there is no limit or measure; that is worship." The use of praise and worship to God is not simple showing of reverence to God. It is a system of transformation. It can lift a person above any circumstance, and let God's miraculous power flow. The shouts used in praise and worship can be so powerful that it can bind the devil with chains that will never let loose of him. The shout of victory is the most powerful expression of praise and worship to God.

When in league with the Holy Spirit, praise and worship can take people above any circumstances, and can also bring about a new level in the spiritual realm. Jesus said in John 14:26, *"But the helper, the Holy Spirit, whom the Father will send in my name, He will teach you all things and bring to your remembrance all that I have said to you."* When Jesus walked on the earth, He was fully human as much as He was fully divine.

He was to operate on the level of a human. He worked, prayed, gave thanks to God, went to temple (synagogue), and kept the rituals and commandments that the Jewish people lived by. He also operated on the act of fulfilling the laws of God and becoming more than what people were at that time before the fulfillment of the price of sin. Once He had paid the price of sin on the cross, it would be time for humans to operate on a new level with God and with themselves. It was more than His duty to die on the cross, for it was His responsibility to teach people how to live under the new covenant that He would make with them (the fulfilled covenant of salvation). That was one of the reasons that He operated within the authority of the Holy Spirit, which was to teach how to live the full existence of being one with God and in relationship to Him.

Like Lucifer, humanity had a voice with God through the Holy Spirit. They had a way to operate in the spiritual realm with God Himself manifested in His Holy Spirit. It was His comfort which was given to us through the Holy Spirit.

Paul writes in Romans 8:26 on the intercession of the Holy Spirit that, *"Likewise the spirit helps us in our weakness. For we do not know what to pray for as we ought to, but the spirit Himself intercedes for us with groaning too deep for words."* The Holy Spirit is a comforter and guide from God. I Corinthians 2:13 states, *"And we impart this in words taught not by human wisdom but taught by the spirit, interpreting spiritual truths to those who are spiritual."* During a church service's praise and worship or during a healing service, there is often a time when the worship can come to a very deep place.

If the worship is pure and true, the Holy Spirit will move throughout the congregation and often move people to speak in tongues, say words of prophecy, sing songs from the spirit, and other things that are manifested from the movement of the Holy Spirit. The Holy Spirit will make a service, or more specifically a group of people experience wonders that they have never known, seen, or spoken before.

Worship is a form of the creations respect to the Creator. Musicians and singers create songs and praises to God with words of respect, glory, and honor. Singers gather their voices together to sing praises to Him as a single unified voice. Is this not a more perfect atmosphere for the Holy Spirit to move in, to bring about new beginnings and healings in people's lives?

The Holy Spirit is the key to bringing about the flow of God through praise and worship. The very essence of the Holy Spirit is the same as worship itself, that of wonder! The Holy Spirit is also primal in many respects. Think of Him from these points of view. It was the Holy Spirit who was with God in the very beginning before time itself began. He was there when Lucifer first was the angel of worship, and then the fallen adversary to God. If all knowledge and creation comes from God, then so too does it originate from the Holy Spirit who is God. All things before they come into existence are already in the Holy Spirit's thoughts and heart. As the Creator, when worship is played, then the spirit of the Creator moves in harmony with worship. In a way, it could be viewed as an atmosphere similar to the atmosphere in which creation was made.

In Ezekiel 36:26-27, Ezekiel gives testimony of God saying, *"And I will give you a new heart, and a new spirit I will put within you. And I will remove the heart of stone from your flesh and give you a heart of flesh. And I will put my spirit within you, and cause you to work in my statutes and be careful to obey my rules."* The Prophet Ezekiel, whose name means "whom God strengthens," had an amazing insight into the realm of the spirit. His book could be viewed as not only a book of prophecy, but also a guide to the intricacies and lives of those responsible for praise and worship.

As human beings, it is difficult to see the things that are not seen. It requires a view with eyes of faith to see the things that are not either seen or known. In a movement of the Holy Spirit, we must view His movements as a firm believer that operates in the faith that is all knowing. Hebrews 11:27 gives testimony of Moses stating, *"By faith he left Egypt, not being afraid of the anger of the king, for he endured as seeing Him who is invisible."* This is another element of the Holy Spirit that enlists Him to move when He is needed, the gift of faith.

The gifts of the spirit that manifest are ones brought on by the invisible qualities of the Holy Spirit. John 6:3 quotes Jesus saying, *"It is the spirit who gives life; the flesh is no help at all. The words that I have spoken to you are spirit and life."* Now, this verse gives the answer to another of the tools of faith that give the Holy Spirit the chance to flow in faith. This tool is perhaps more powerful than sight by faith, which is faith by hearing. To hear the words of God is the beginning to any relationship with God.

We see Paul giving account to this "hearing faith" in Romans 10:17, *"So faith comes from hearing, and hearing through the word of Christ."* Going deeper with scripture from II Corinthians 5:7, *"For we walk by faith, not by sight."* A blind man, who can't see with natural eyes, trains himself to know his steps by walking with a cane, a dog, or by learning to hear the sounds around him.

Ludwig Van Beethoven, the great German composer of classical music, went deaf after the age of 26 as a result of tinnitus, or ringing in the ear. Although his career as a conductor suffered from his loss of hearing, which he concluded after performing Piano Concerto No. 5 in 1811, he did not stop writing or playing music. To compensate for his loss of hearing, he would use books and notepads to communicate and read music. He would also use various methods and techniques for hearing music through sounds made by vibrations. There are theories that he would saw off the legs of pianos and place them on the ground so he could put his ear to the floor to hear the different sounds made from the vibrations of the different key strokes played.

Another theory is that there was a special piano made that had a covering over the keys so he could place his ear over it and listen to the key strokes from above them. Whatever methods Beethoven used to continue his career as a musician and composer, it is apparent that he did not let the loss of physical sound stop him. He continued to make beautiful music through the words he read, and the invisible sounds that only he was able to hear.

While praise and worship is not merely music, it is still perfectly manifested through music. The examples of Beethoven are evident that music is not simply done with the sounds that we hear from mere instruments. In fact, there are a great many things that can be used to create both music and praise to God. Though he had lost his position as chief worshiper, Lucifer at one time was an angel of so many amazing authorities. He could create worship in a place that time and space were play things for which he could manipulate to make amazing forms of praise and worship to God. These are the gifts that the Holy Spirit works best. The Holy Spirit is the Living God that created everything. Like God the Father, God the Son, and the Holy Spirit is also the Living Word.

In the heavenly realm, there is no more powerful a place than the throne room of God. The very seat that God resides on is one of a being who has so much power in Him that to move could possibly bring about destruction of the entire universe. This is also the seat of the living Word. Hebrews gives description of the word of God as, *"For the word of God is living and active, sharper than any two edged sword, piercing to the division of the soul and of spirit, of intentions of the heart."*

John 1:14 says, *"And the Word became flesh and dwelt among us, and we have seen His glory, glory as of the only Son from the Father, full of grace and truth."* It is possible to view the trinity of God as God the Father being the spiritual and purest incarnation of the power of the word, which makes up His being. Jesus is then the physical and natural manifestation of the word in flesh and blood, the walking, talking version of God and the word as man. The Holy Spirit could then be seen as the sound of God, the unseen words spoken, and the unseen presence moving in the natural through the supernatural.

Let's look at a lesson on the different levels of the speeds of God based on thought, light, and sound. Although it is believed that light is to be considered the fastest of speeds, I would say that the speed of thought was actually the fastest. God's first thought could be considered the first thing ever to come into existence since in the beginning there was nothing but God.

Let us imagine for a moment what existence was like before what we could consider life or even before creation came into being. Picture there being nothing before nothing even was in existence. No light, sound, thought, and not even darkness. All there is being God, God without form, and completely devoid of what we define as being, and He simply (at this time before time) "is." He is the perfect example of what was, is, and is to come as described in Revelation 1:4, 1:8, and 4:8. Then, for the first time in what would become history, a single thought was made. This thought becomes the first words of the word of God. From there, the rest of creation as we see throughout the teachings in the Bible comes into being.

This is the essence of the Holy Spirit. He is the thing not seen, the flowing of God in the presence of worship from the Creation to the Creator. He is the sound that is spoken in the ears of the people that are willing to listen to His voice, for it is the voice of God that is speaking. When in worship to the Creator, The Holy Spirit is the presence of God in the room manifested for the signs and wonders of heaven and earth. The very songs and voices heard are exalted by Him and the Father above. Psalm

46:10 says, *"Be still, and know that I am God. I will be exalted among the nations, and I will be exalted in the earth!"* Praise and worship could not really be praise and worship without a real movement of the spirit with the Holy Spirit.

Those who would not seek God or the Holy Spirit would not have the spiritual manifestation needed to promote healing, restoration, or messages from the spirit. Hebrews 11:6 states, *"And without faith, it is impossible to please Him, for whoever would draw near to God must believe that He exists and that He rewards those who seek Him."* How can you be filled with the Holy Spirit and fire if you don't seek Him? To seek out the Holy Spirit is the same as seeking Jesus, for it was Christ who gave the Holy Spirit to us in the first place. The Holy Spirit is the fullness of God as described in Ephesians 3:19, *"And to know this love that surpasses knowledge-that you may be filled to the measure of all the fullness of God."* He is the sound, the voice of God heard on earth.

When understanding the nature of praise and worship, it is important to remember that the Holy Spirit is the essential key to the praise and worship of and to God. As voices ring high to God, it is the flowing of the Holy Spirit that makes the voice, the presence of God flowing into, around, and through people for whatever reasons they are seeking the Father. The movement of the spirit of God in worship is transformed to its purest form that God had originally planned it to be. Romans 12:2, *"Do not be conformed to this world, but transformed by the renewal of your mind, that by testing you may discern what is the will of God, what is good and acceptable and perfect."*

An example of being transformed in the spirit can be seen in Acts 2:4 on the Day of Pentecost, *"And they were all filled with the Holy Spirit and began to speak in other tongues as the spirit gave them utterance."* The invisible flowing of the Holy Spirit is an atmosphere of transformation and renewing. The sounds uttered by Him are from the very throne room of God the Father. The sounds of God are available 24/7 to the people of God. It only takes the desire to listen to them, to let them flow, and to let the Holy Spirit lead you that will make God's sounds become alive to the worshiper of God.

Chapter Three

The Holy Spirit, Spiritual
Sounds, and the Living Temple

Both in the natural and supernatural realms there is a movement of the spirit that resonates with sound. The interaction with the sound depends on the role that the sound is playing. What is important though is that all things work together with sound. As music is the language of the universe, so too is sound a holding fabric of life itself. The word of God in fact can be defined through sound.

In John 1:1 it says, *"In the beginning was the Word, and the Word was with God, and the Word was God."* In the last chapter we discussed the Holy Spirit being the unseen word of God that is spoken into each and every believer's ear. This would then put the Holy Spirit as the word of God in the purest form of the word that is spoken, heard, and felt in the heart and spirit. As an unseen voice to the world, the Holy Spirit is best described as God's word incarnate.

It is difficult to identify every single part of the God head as the roles and nature of the Holy Trinity is infinite and mysterious. We do know that the existence of God, Jesus, and the Holy Spirit within the Trinity is an arrangement of all together as one body, and yet operate separate from each other as individuals. To identify the Holy Spirit as the Living word of God, unseen but spoken, is a description depicted due to the nature of the word in which He operates in on earth. To identify (in theory) that the Holy Spirit is the word manifested, unlike God, the Father, and Jesus, the Son, who are also the word manifested, but walk in physical forms, is based on the sacredness and reverence the Bible makes for the Holy Spirit.

Though not often worshipped or praised like father God or Jesus, the Holy Spirit is to be respected and more importantly, not sinned against. The sinning against the Holy Spirit is laid out in Matthew 12:31, *"Therefore I tell you, every sin and blasphemy will be forgiven people, but the blasphemy against the spirit will not be forgiven."* Continued into Matthew 12:32 we read, *"And whoever speaks a word against the Son of Man will be forgiven, but whoever speaks against the Holy Spirit will not be forgiven, be in this age or in the age to come."*

As stated in Matthew, you can sin and ask forgiveness from God, but to sin against the Holy Spirit is unforgiveable. The examples from the verses of Matthew show that the Holy Spirit is not only on an equal level of importance with God and Jesus, but that how you respect or sin against Him is a very serious matter! Taken the wrong way, offenses are unforgiveable toward the Holy Spirit He must then be revered, or risk the consequences of God being unforgiving.

Out of the many reasons that it is vital to avoid sinning against the Holy Spirit, one of the more relevant reasons could be due to His nature as the "Holy" Spirit. I John 5:6 states, *"This is He who came by water and blood-Jesus Christ; not by the water only but by the water and the blood. And the spirit is the one who testifies, because the spirit is the truth."* While on the earth as man, Jesus operated outside of His godly status as creator God, choosing instead to walk as God's created man.

While He was still very much God, Jesus operated within the gifts of the Holy Spirit to lead and guide Him in His everyday life. His miracles, teachings, knowledge and power all were done in league with the Holy Spirit. This was done to teach and prepare mankind for when the Holy Spirit would become available to them once the work of Jesus had been finished. Jesus said that He would leave behind a helper for His children once He ascended to heaven. That helper is the Holy Spirit. Being part of the God head, both Jesus and the Holy Spirit are of the same divine nature. As Jesus is the way, the truth, and the life, so too is the Holy Spirit.

Mark 3:22-30 says, *"Truly, I say to you, all sins will be forgiven the children of man, and whatever blasphemies they utter, but whoever blasphemes against the Holy Spirit never has forgiveness, but is guilty of an eternal sin"-for they were saying, "He has an unclean spirit."* To sin against the Holy Spirit is to invite sin into the holiness of the Holy Spirit, and since there is no sin in God, then there can't be in the Holy Spirit. The spirit of God must remain holy and pure, and it is with this awareness of the pure holy nature of the Holy Spirit that we see what atmosphere is manifested in the pure moves of the spirit in praise and worship.

The spirit of God can be said to be the purest dwelling place of true praise and worship. When a movement of the spirit takes place, it takes worshipers into a far deeper place in the spirit. It is in this place that is now holy ground that signs and wonders can take place, where God's power can be seen and manifested, and where miracles can happen.

The flow of the spirit is one of the most powerful manifestations of the presence of God. In the ancient times of the Old Testament, they were often seen and described in detail as images of amazing signs and wonders. When the presence of the Lord was revealed to Moses in the mountains as a burning bush, God then declared the area as holy ground and instructed Moses to remove his shoes to show reverence to its sanctity. When King Saul was tormented by an evil spirit and David would play his songs of praise, the atmosphere would welcome the presence of the Lord to which would grant King Saul peace and rest. In the lifetime of the Apostle Paul, the worship and praises that he would sing to God while in prison would become so powerful that the prison would shake to the point that the iron doors would open to them. The presence of the spirit of God in praise and worship creates an atmosphere like that in Moses day that is considered holy ground. The songs of praise that go up to the throne room of God can cause demons and chains to fall.

John 4:23 reads, *"But the hour is coming, and is now here, when the true worshipers will worship the Father in spirit and truth, for the Father is seeking such people to worship Him."* All praise to God is welcomed to Him, but only a flow of the Holy Spirit is when His presence can be truly felt. John 4:24 states, *"God is spirit, and those who worship Him must worship in spirit and in truth."* As the Holy Spirit is part of God's perfect nature, then all things that are done with Him must be done in the understanding of seeking that which is perfect in the eyes of God. That which is perfect with Him in regards to praise and worship is the perfect atmosphere that will allow His perfect nature, His perfect truth, and His perfect healing power to manifest and come alive in all those that seek to worship Him.

The word of the Lord is perfect, and that makes the Holy Spirit a perfect spirit. His perfect nature gives the atmosphere of praise that gift of making a healing atmosphere, a knowledge and wisdom atmosphere, and an atmosphere that will give any who are willing to receive the gifts of the Holy Spirit the presence in which their faith can receive, because they believed, received, and approached God as He desires and requires in His presence on holy ground.

What is necessary for the Holy Spirit to operate in the atmosphere of holy ground is a sacrifice from the people seeking the presence of God. That sacrifice is the surrender of a person to the perfect will of God. I Chronicles 16:29 states, *"Ascribe to the Lord the glory due*

His name; bring an offering and come before Him! Worship the Lord in the splendor of holiness."

While music and voice are instruments to be used in worship to God, it is the spiritual sounds of the spirit that will make a worshiper feel a sense of wonder to the creator. That is the power of God, and that is the voice of the Holy Spirit; the sound of God's word. This atmosphere is triggered by the voices shouting to Him in one accord or voice.

In Psalm 149:3 it reads, *"Let them praise His name with dancing, making melody to Him with tambourine and lyre!"* I Chronicles 25:6 reads, *"They were all under the direction of their father in the music in the house of the Lord with cymbals, harps, and lyres for the service of the house of God."* The key words to these scriptures are the words 'they' and 'them.' When the voices of the people worshiping were in one accord of praise, then that was when the atmosphere was blessed with the presence of God manifested. Like on the Day of Pentecost when the disciples were all speaking in tongues and saw tongues above their heads, so too is the atmosphere when the praises to God are sung by those with the spirit of God in their lives and His praise on their lips.

When the atmosphere has become holy, then not only will the Holy Spirit be able to provide an atmosphere of healing and salvation, but also one of knowledge and understanding. Colossians 3:16 reads, *"Let the Word of Christ dwell in you richly, teaching and admonishing one another in all wisdom, singing psalms and hymns and spiritual songs, with thankfulness in your hearts to God."* The word of God will come alive in a person who has accepted the Holy Spirit into his life. He will guide them in wisdom and open them up to the speaking and interpretation of their spiritual language or tongues as it is also known.

This language of the spirit, the language of tongues, is described in I Corinthians 14:2, *"For one who speaks in a tongue speaks not to men but to God; for no one understands him, but he utters mysteries in the Spirit."* The Holy Spirit will open the spiritual gifts of a person to be able to speak with languages that they never knew they could speak. The words that will flow from the mouths will be words of the spirit often as words of prophecy and wisdom.

Each speaking of tongues and the interpretations given are unique to each and every person. While the voice of the people is to be sung in one accord, the unique gifts, needs, and desires of each voice is still unique to the presence of the Holy Spirit and will then open up each individual to their own opportunity in the spirit. I Corinthians 14:4 states, *"The one who speaks in a tongue builds up himself, but the one who prophesies builds up the church."*

While each individual has their own unique gifts in the spirit, the flow of the spirit is always stronger when done in a majority. The spiritual sounds made by one voice's majority will always have a profound effect on those that operate in God's oneness. Those that seek to understand this truth will see the results as God allows them to unfold when the truth is ready to be revealed.

During the We Who Worship Gathering held by Salem Family Ministries in 2012, Cheryl Salem, my beloved mother, gave a sermon on the different levels of sounds that open up the spirit. During one of her sermons, she had the entire audience sing a simple music note in unison. That simple note flowed so well that there was an immediate feeling of peace and harmony within the room that the event was being held in. It was almost as if a small opening to the heavenly realm had been opened because of this frequency of unified sound.

Her reason behind this demonstration was to point out that there is a unique flow within the spiritual realm when the voices of those seeking to worship God approach Him in one accord. The melodies sung can produce an entrance for the flowing of the Holy Spirit. Matthew 18:20 reads, *"For where two or more are gathered in my name, there I am among you."*

I Corinthians 6:19, *"Or do you not know that your body is a temple of the Holy Spirit within you, whom you have from God? You are not your own."* When you allow Jesus to enter your life, and allow for the Holy Spirit to enter and flow in you, then you open yourself to become the holy temple for Jesus just as the tabernacle and Solomon's temple once were His dwelling places. This means that you are now the holy place for God to dwell. As there was worship in the tabernacle and temple, your voice is the worship to the God who lives in you. John 7:38 says, *"Whoever believes in Me, as the scripture said, 'Out of his heart will flow rivers of living water.'"* As Jesus comes to live inside of you, so then everything that flows from you becomes alive and is entwined with the very spirit of God who now resides with you.

Chapter Four

Worship and Praise from the
Living Temple of God

The Lord works through those who choose to follow and honor Him. Matthew 10:20 states, *"For it's not you who speak, but the spirit of your Father speaking through you."* When you accept Jesus into your life, your body then becomes the temple for which He will come to live. As such, God will then begin to work through you and lead you for you have given Him control of your life. This makes you a living instrument for God as the Apostle Paul was during his lifetime.

For the longest time in the Old Testament, God had a dwelling place in the tabernacle in the wilderness during the time of the judges, and then in the temple of Solomon.

after the establishment of Israeli monarchial rule. The word tabernacle is Latin in origin for tabernaculum meaning tent or hut. In Hebrew the word is Mishkan which means residence or dwelling place. The temple of Solomon is referred to as the holy temple or Bet Hamikdash in Hebrew. There are 4 temples mentioned in the Bible starting with Solomon's temple, and ending with the temple of God that resides in heaven (the original that the other temples on earth are modeled after) found in Revelation 11:19. The true temple of God though is not made of stone, but of flesh and blood.

It is a living temple where the spirit of God dwells. I Corinthians 3:16-17 tells us, *"Do you not know that you are God's temple and that God's spirit dwells in you? If anyone destroys God's temple, God will destroy him. For God's temple is holy, and you are that temple."* The very body that you were born with that keeps your own spirit is the same temple where God Himself dwells. This is why it is important to obey the laws and commandments of God. To keep your temple pure and to live a godly life is to honor the temple that the creator of the universe dwells.

The relevance of praise and worship in league with a living temple is because when you sing to God, you make living worship. People sing praises to God in a church or building, but your very body is a living temple that gives God one of a kind worship from the depths of a sacred dwelling place. A perfect example of how you are a living temple for God can be seen in Psalm 51.

Out of the Psalms to God, the 51st is perhaps the most instructive as it is beautiful in describing living the right way for God, to being sacred in your steps to God, and showing how your body is a tool for worship to Him. The Psalm reads as:

Be generous, God, in Your kindness; in Your great mercy, erase what I did.
Wash me clean of my misdeed, purify me of my sin.
For I know that I did wrong. My sin is always on my mind.
You are the one I offended; I did what is evil in Your sight.
You always are fair in Your sentence, impartial in what You decree.
But consider, I was born to transgression, conceived by my mother in sin.
Secretly You love faithfulness; so in secret help me grow wise.
Clean me with hyssop till I am pure, wash me till I'm whiter than snow.
Let me have gladness and joy once again, let the bones that You struck rejoice.
Turn away from my sin, and blot out all my offenses.
God, make me a pure heart, put a new, right spirit inside me.
Please, don't send me away; don't take Your Holy Spirit from me.
Give me back the joy of Your help, hold me up with a kindly spirit.
Let me teach sinners Your ways, so offenders may turn back to You.
God, my salvation, save me from death, so I can celebrate Your kindness.
Open my lips, O Lord, and my mouth will declare Your presence.
You don't want any sacrifice I could give; You have no desire for offerings.
God's sacrifices are a chastened spirit, a chastened broken heart God will not reject.

And in Your favor be good Zion, rebuild Jerusalem's walls.
Then true sacrifices will be Your delight, whole and burnt.
Offerings; then let the sacrificial animals go up to Your
altars.

Though it does speak of forgiveness, it is the declarations of "the bones rejoicing," and the "opening of lips to declare your presence" that exemplify the worship that comes forth from the human temple of God.

The poetry of the 51st Psalm shows the way that a person worships God with the respect and honor. God never asks for great and mighty things for Himself. The only things He has ever asked of people are that they love Him, obey His commandments, and follow His laws that He has set out in order for people to live their lives to the fullest. He never complained about a temple for His presence to dwell in or a giant cathedral from which worship was to ring out to Him.

In the Old Testament, God dwelt in a tent while the Israelites were in the desert. In the later years of Israel the praises to God from a simple shepherd boy were enough to declare that shepherd, who is King David, a man after God's own heart. In the New Testament, God spoke not only in the temple, but in the wilderness, from the top of a hill, and from the sea. The songs of praise and worship of Paul and Silas while in a prison cell were so great that the prison itself shook in awe from the power of God. It is not buildings of stone and metal, or places that are called sacred that make a place holy for God. It is the presence of the Lord and His dwelling or resting over a place that make it holy ground.

II Corinthians 6:16 the scripture declares, *"What agreement has the temple of God with idols? For we are the temple of the living God; as God said, "I will make my dwelling among them and walk among them, and I will be their God, and they shall be My people."* It seems obvious that God prefers His own creation as the temple for Him to dwell. As an individual creation we are given a voice made to speak to the ends of the world, stated in Psalm 19:4, *"Yet their voice goes out into all the earth, their words to the ends of the world."* This would undoubtedly be the most unique and precious kind of temple to the creator since that same temple also shares traits with its creator. That is, the creation that man shares traits with its creator, which is God.

This is seen in Genesis 1:26, *"Let us make man in Our image, after Our likeness,"* and again in the following verse of Genesis 1:27, *"So God created man in His own image, in the image of God He created him; male and female He created them."* God is the creator and architect not only of a temple fearfully and wonderfully made, but also of a temple that is similar to His very being.

To be a living temple for God begins when we accept Jesus Christ into our lives. Once He comes into a life upon receiving salvation, He can begin rebuilding the temple where God now resides. The work of rebuilding this temple that is man in the form of a living temple has been witnessed by some of the most prominent ministers and musicians in the modern age. Among them is my mother, Cheryl Salem.

In her book Rebuilding The Ruins of Worship Cheryl goes into detail about the subject of praise and worship. Her research has been extensive for this book, and has shown deep devotion to the explanations of praise and worship to God. In her book starting with the first chapter entitled "Rebuilding the Ruins of Worship" given instruction on how worship is a form of deep communication to God. For this communication to God, Cheryl says that in order to begin we must have the correct form of "thinking" when worshiping. She says in detail that, "We must learn how to 'think" correctly if we are to be correct. We must be able to willingly go into the fire of purification if we are to attain the depths intended for purity that worship is to afford. Worship is about integrity, purity, and accountability. Worship is not about the use of your gifts or talents. Don't get me wrong, God loves the gifted and talented who are willing to lay it all down at His feet and be used for His glory. This is the perfect scenario of a worshiper; one who is gifted and talented and totally submitted to His will. But ultimately, I believe God will use the less gifted that are totally submitted and yielded above the more gifted who still think worship is about the worshiper rather than the One who is being worshiped!"

This quote from Cheryl gives the perfect example of how a worshiper is to be submitted to the creator God who lives within them. To allow Him to use you for whatever purposes He has planned for you and His living temple in which He lives is your sole purpose.

Jesus Himself was an instrument of the Father when He walked the earth. Though He is God, Jesus operated on the same levels as humans do with God. His gifts were manifested by the Holy Spirit that operated within Him.

Jesus was an example of the interactions between man and the Holy Spirit. When He would depart back to heaven, humanity would then have the knowledge of how to interact with the Holy Spirit individually and together. John 5:30 finds Jesus saying, *"I can do nothing on my own. As I hear, I judge, and my judgment is just, because I seek not my own will but the will of Him who sent me."* As a man, He let Himself be moved by the spirit, submitted to the Father's will, and operated as the Father saw fit for Him. This is made evident further on the Mount of Olives before the crucifixion.

Before going to the cross, Jesus is preparing Himself for what will happen to Him on the cross and the events leading up to it. In a brief moment of His alone time with God He asks God if there is another way for the payment of sin to be made. Luke 22:42 reads, *"Father, if you are willing, remove this cup from me."* For one time, as all man does, Jesus tried to seek another way to do something, even though it was prophetically the only way it could happen. Then, it reads further, "Nevertheless, not my will, *but* yours, be done." Though He didn't want the crucifixion to happen (who would honestly), Jesus was putting God and His will first, and put Himself second in order to be the perfect sacrifice for sin and imperfect man. Jesus set it all on the line for God to use Him as was needed. This is what He expects for all humans to do when they come to Him in worship and all other matters of walking with God in your life.

The definition of worship in Old English etymology is defined as "worthiness or worth-ship; to give, at its simplest, worth to something." The simplest thing we can ever give to God is ourselves. What is available to us individually more than anything is our right to "choice," our "free-will." The one thing that God has given us that is the greatest gift is our free will. He wants people to choose freely to come to Him, to listen to Him, and to let Him lead you. This is the reason that God has given us the Bible, salvation, and the Holy Spirit. II Timothy 3:16 tells us, *"All scripture is breathed out by God and profitable for teaching, for reproof, for correction, and for training in righteousness."* This is the same with our praise and worship to Him.

Let us look at praise and worship in another light. All forms of music are beautiful. A piano, a guitar, a drum set, and a voice all can have individual sounds, types of performances, and wonderful sounds that come from them that are amazing. When put together in a band, orchestra, or chorus, these instruments can become flawless works of beauty when heard.

Individually, a person's voice or instrument playing can be great to hear. People who choose to sing songs to God, or play music to Him can be very talented and moving. Now add God into the mix of this music. Imagine the flowing of a band, a praise team, or a choir with Him. The flow of the music then becomes much more penetrating to the individual, deeper flowing. This creates the atmosphere of praise and worship that true believers seek when they desire to worship God, to receive from Him everything that needs to be sought.

Hebrews 4:16 says, *"Let us then with confidence draw near to the throne of grace, that we may receive mercy and find grace to help in time of need."* We must do so with faith and belief in God. Hebrews 11:6 reads, *"And without faith it is impossible to please Him, for whoever would draw near to God must believe that He exists and that He rewards those who seek Him."* If we are saved by grace by our belief in Him, then when we worship God, we must believe that something will come forth from our worship. We worship not for ourselves, but for the God of Creation. When we worship God with a spirit of pure praise and worship to Him, God then begins to wash over us.

Pure worship is like a purifying bath that washes all over us, removing the stains of sin, opening the heart, and making the believer pure in the sight of God. Hebrews 10:22 reads, *"Let us draw near with a true heart in full assurance of faith, with our hearts sprinkled clean from an evil conscience and our bodies washed with pure water."* The presence of God when manifested will cleanse and wipe away all the things that were bad in a person's life. The presence of God will also give and reveal things to a person when He manifests.

I Corinthians 14:16 has taught us about a deep revelation through worshiping together. It reads, *"What then, brothers? When you come together, each one has a hymn, a lesson, a revelation, a tongue, or an interpretation. Let all things be done for building up."* There are things that each and every one of us in the world are seeking for themselves with God. Those that know the living God are always searching for the things that God sends to help them. When we ask God for help, He will answer but in His own way. We often wish for things to be answered or resolved based on how we wish it to happen. Once in a blue moon, God will do things as we think it will happen. More often than not though, what God has planned for our answers will be done in a completely different way. When we ask God into our lives, we are His to guide as He sees fit.

Romans 14:8 states, *"For if we live, we live to the Lord, and if we die, we die to the Lord. So then, whether we live or whether we die, we are the Lord's."* What we ask of God is then done according to God's will. When we ask Him for guidance, we are His. When we seek His help, we are His. Whatever we ask of God will be done His way, and like in praise and worship, we must submit to His authority on the matter and let Him handle it His way.

The movement of the spirit in praise and worship can produce the exact things that a person is in need from God. What we seek can be manifested from the throne room of God in a pure atmosphere of praise. Many times in churches having a pure move of the spirit, there will be a time where revelation will come to the worshiper. The words of the Father will be spoken through someone who God chooses to speak through. Sometimes it can be heard through one or more individuals at a time depending on how the Holy Spirit chooses to move.

Answers individually can be felt at times in the spirit of people when they are worshiping God. The best explanation to this feeling of knowledge is because a person lets go of their worries, gives it to God, and the comfort of the Holy Spirit will come over them. The cleansing of the person can be done from the pure waters of God for these waters are living waters from the throne room of God.

Healing can take place during pure worship to God. The need for healing from anything, whether it be physical, mental, or any other forms can take place. The prophet Isaiah gives testament to Gods healing power in Isaiah 41:10, *"Fear not, for I am with you; be not dismayed for I am your God; I will strengthen you, I will help you, I will uphold you with my righteous right hand."* In Jeremiah 17:14, the prophet Jeremiah gives admittance of healing through praise, *"Heal me, O Lord, and I shall be healed; save me, and I shall be saved, for you are my 'Praise.'"* Jeremiah also gives account to healing in other forms besides the physical. Jeremiah 33:6 states, *"Behold, I will bring health and healing, and I will heal them and reveal to them abundance of prosperity and security."*

The minor prophets of the Old Testament are individuals who understood the yoke of God's power. Many of them were tested again and again in all matters of God's power through the physical, mental, and spiritual. Their knowledge expanded into the realms of revelations of the future, intimacy with the Father, healing and manifestation of the gifts and answers from God, and the interactions of the spirit through praise and worship. While their works are not all on praise and worship, their words and experiences in their time in the presence of God reveal knowledge of deep understanding, and words of wisdom, knowledge, and truth from the Father Himself.

The prophets were unique in their interactions with God the Father. This is perhaps due to the unique nature in which they walked with God. Unlike other people, prophets had an interaction with God that was based not on simply seeking God, but from God speaking to them at His pleasure and on His (God's) time. They were His ambassadors to humanity, and were on call to Him 24/7.

Their interactions with God were done in total obedience to God, surrender to His will, and allowing Him to flow through them as the living God who works signs and wonders. Amos 3:7 reads, *"For the Lord God does nothing without revealing His secrets to His servants the prophets."* What would we really understand about interacting with the spirit of God without the prophets that God had given to us? How could we know what His divine will was, or how prophecy was spoken through man from the very mouth of God? How could we have learned about anointing without first seeing those who were anointed of God? It is clear that the prophets are an example of how the movement of the spirit in this day and age through praise and worship can be almost exactly like it was in the days of the prophets of the Bible.

All the miracles and wonders that God did through His prophets can also be seen now through any individual who the anointing falls on when the spirit of God moves. This is made evident in II Peter 1:21, *"For no prophecy was ever produced by the will of man, but men spoke from God as they were carried along by the Holy Spirit."*

The word of the Lord is like a flowing river that spreads through people when it can flow freely. With prophets, it was through a spirit of willingness and obedience (albeit some prophets had a harder time than others agreeing to do Gods work such as Moses and Jonah). With worshipers, it is the free flowing of the spirit in the midst of pure praise and worship that allows God to move over the congregation and people gathered. Hebrews 1:1-2 gives account to the prophets and worshipers' anointing stating, *"Long ago, at many times and in many ways, God spoke to our fathers by the prophets, but in these last days He has spoken to us by His Son, who He appointed the heir of all things, through whom He also created the world."*

The Lord's anointing is the greatest feeling that can be felt in praise and worship. In no less than a moment it can wash over you and completely consume you. If you are is feeling weary, tired, or stressed, the flow of the anointing can feel renewing to your spirit. It can energize you and give you a feeling of joy, relaxation, and rest. This is what God intended for people with Him and the flow of His spirit.

We read in Matthew 11:28-30, *"Come to Me, all who labor and are heavy laden, and I will give you rest. Take My yoke upon you, and learn from Me, for I am gentle and lowly in heart, and you will find rest for your souls. For My yoke is easy, and My burden is light."* This is what will happen in the flow of the spirit at the height of praise and worship, and it is this feeling that everyone who worships should strive for during any service or private time with the Lord.

Chapter Five

Being the Living Temple
with the Imprinted Heart

My whole life has been one of travel and work in ministry. Ever since I was a little boy, I had been taught to sing, to learn music, and how to worship God. My mother, Cheryl Salem, would have me, my brother Roman, and my sister Gabrielle practice and learn music for hours. As a professional singer, an ordained minister, and an educated teacher with double majors in music and teaching, we could not have asked for a better or more qualified person to teach us.

When I was beginning to sing, the routines to learn music and singing were simple. We would be taught how to know our voices pitch, range, and other vocal talents. In solo music I would sing a lot of my mother's earlier songs that were easy and fun. In a group we would sing simple songs like Jesus Loves Me, and a few other songs that were appropriate for young singers.

As I got older, the training began to become more serious and dedicated. When my sister went home to be with God, I sang solo for a few years. When we grew older, our music stopped being less individual and started to become more group based.

Our music began to get deeper as we sang songs that were slower and based on intimate worship. We sang songs such as 'The Mercy Seat' and 'Pour My Love on You' in our services. This type of music presented an atmosphere of worship that was different to me. While I was aware of the spirit of God in my life, I never really grew up with this type of movement in the spirit.

I grew up learning to listen to the voice of God, but the flow of the Holy Spirit was something that only happened on certain occasions such as when I would speak in tongues, or lay hands on people in moments of healing during a service. There was a feeling when I did it that felt like a wave of serious energy flowing through me. As a kid, the feeling of the Holy Spirit as I laid my hands on people felt so exciting to me. It was interesting to watch people fall under the healing power of God just by a simple touch of my hand on their forehead or body. It was cool to be able to do something like 'put people under the healing power of God' just like the ministers I would watch on television. It gave me the sense of wonder and awe that I still get to this day when I imagine all of the amazing powers that the creator of the universe is capable of doing through humans.

My point for mentioning these memories is based on three important things. The first is that as a kid, I was trained to know how to sing, understand music, and to know the music of praise and worship. The second is that I was always listening to the spirit, being open to it, and willing to be used as the Lord saw fit. The third was that I had an understanding of the flow of the spirit from my first two experiences which enabled me to continue to evolve in my walk with God. My gifts in Him were able to develop farther and deeper, giving me a desire and conviction to expand my knowledge of God, the Holy Spirit, and other areas significantly.

At a young age, I gave my heart to God after seeing a play that involved a young woman being cast out of heaven for God did not know her. That night after I saw the play, I was scared for my own salvation and immediately gave my heart to God. Being a young boy upon seeing this play, which was quite stirring to me, it took me some time to fully digest that I was now saved and belonged to God. My grandmother and my parents were there to comfort and to help me understand that since I gave my heart to God, I had nothing to fear. I was a new creature in Christ Jesus. As it says in II Corinthians 5:17, *"Therefore, if any man be in Christ, he is a new creature."*

Being young when this happened, I was able to grow with my childhood into my life with God. Many times when we are born again, the life that we attain with God is one that we have to learn and grow. With my life in Christ being started at a young age, I was able to grow gradually and carefully. I read my Bible, watched TV shows based on Bible stories, ministers and preachers with many different messages and testimonies, and read books and articles on God and theology. Though I was growing in knowledge and faith through my studies, the learning and fascination of the spirit came from my mother.

My mother, Cheryl Salem, was the best role model I had in my life to learn about the Holy Spirit and the workings of the spirit. She is a strong Christian, and has a great love of God. It was the warmth I felt from spending time with her as a kid that made me desire to learn from her.

I was a wild kid in my youth, and was always getting into some kind of crazy adventure. This I believe, made my mother quite exhausted at the day's end. Even so, she was never too busy to answer a question I had about God. She would read to us at night, sing to us, and she would always pray with us until we got old enough to pray ourselves. When she began to teach us music, it was a lot of effort to learn on our part. We had to be taught like in school with a type of music curriculum.

She would have us learn our voice pitches first; how high, how low, how long we could hold a note, how to use vibrato, and to straighten our voices. She would have us sing individually for about an hour or so, sometimes with the piano to hear different keys and melodies. She would sometimes teach us little dance numbers or movements to go with the songs so we would not be completely stiff on stage. She would also encourage us to sing in the spirit and to just let the spirit flow through our music if we felt the anointing anytime during our songs.

I learned from reading my mother's book, <u>A Bright Shining Place,</u> that she was aware of the Holy Spirit and the anointing of God at a very young age. After a car accident that left her with a shorter left leg than her right one, my mother went to a healing crusade one night held by an evangelist whose name was Kenneth Hagin. After believing for her healing, Kenneth laid his hands on my mother and she was healed miraculously as her left leg grew to the same equal length as her right leg.

From this story, I realized that everything that she was teaching and would teach us would always be in league with understanding of how to hear and flow in the Holy Spirit. We were to be the living temples that God would use to bring about His message, salvation, and work to teach people.

Being in ministry, I was going to have to become an individual who represented God in all things. I was going to need to become someone that people would see an example of someone who God works through, who represents His messages, and who stands in faith for knowing God is always working and delivering everything He promises. I needed to become as it says in Hebrew 8:2, *"A minister in the holy places, in the true tent that the Lord set up, not man."* I needed to also be a pure soul that God could operate through as it states from I Peter 1:2, *"Having purified your souls by your obedience to the truth for a sincere brotherly love, love one another earnestly from a pure heart."* I needed to become the living testament from God to man who lived the godly life, and a living lesson of walking and operating in the Holy Spirit.

While I have sung and ministered in music ministry, my real workings in the spirit have been through trying to understand the many different levels of the spirit that exist. My most favorite scripture that I have taken to heart is from Romans 1:20, *"For His invisible attributes, namely, His eternal power and divine nature, have been clearly perceived, ever since the creation of the world, in the things that have been made. So they (humanity) are without excuse."* Since the scripture shows that God has made His eternal power and divine nature known throughout time, I have attempted to uncover Him from hints and clues of His existence throughout the different cultures and peoples of the world.

There is a great deal of God that is seen in other cultures. Among the many nations that have different ways of life, God has made Himself evident to them in one form or another. In certain cultures that have not had the chance to learn of God from a teacher, a prophet, or the Holy Scriptures, God did make His presence known through their connections to His natural wonders. That is His invisible voice heard in the quiet of the heart and mind.

Among my studies into the different cultures that have had a touch from the creator God, I have seen that Native Americans have had some of the most profound encounters and reverence to the Lord of hosts. To them, He is the 'Great Creator Spirit,' the 'Creator of all life.' While South and Central American Indian tribes created civilizations based around false gods and deities, the Native Americans of North America had a much different view of the supernatural.

When you look at Native American culture, you see that they never actually worship other spirits, save for the Great Spirit that to them is God. They create totem poles with animals on them, but they never worship the animals; only revere them for their sacredness in connection to the land. They have tribal dances to pay respect to creation and all that is in it as a way of honoring the Great Spirit who gave them the land that they use for their daily living. To pay the ultimate respects to the Great Spirit, the many tribes of North America would come together and worship Him.

I paid attention to the many different forms of song and dance that the tribes would use to pay homage to the Great Spirit. Though they may not have used the name God, they did refer to Him as 'Creator.' It was in this title that I realized that not only did God reveal Himself to the peoples of the world through the ways that Romans 1:20 said, but all peoples who believed in a great Creator gave honor to God as an unknown Creator that was nameless to them but known to them.

This could be evidenced through the fact that many nations throughout history were unaware of the existence of who God really was, save for what the Israelites knew of Him through His revealing Himself to them. Through invisible qualities, God showed Himself to the Israelites. He also revealed Himself through physical signs and wonders, His voice spoken plainly, His teachings, and finally His physical manifestations seen throughout the Old Testament right up to His physical birth and life as the Son of man.

We know that God revealed Himself only to a chosen few in the beginning of the Old Testament. After the flood, only a handful of men from Salem (modern day Israel) and Ur (modern day Iraq) were aware of His "Voice;" to hear it, to listen to it, to understand it, to obey it, and take refuge in it. The name of God was rarely known save to those who were open to Him. In Exodus 3:14-15, *"God said to Moses, "I AM that I AM."* And He said,

"Say this to the people of Israel, 'I AM has sent me to you.'"
God also said to Moses, *"Say this to the people of Israel,
'The Lord, the God of your fathers, the God of Abraham,
Isaac, and Jacob, has sent me to you.' This is My name
forever, and thus I am to be remembered throughout all
generations."* This was the gift of God to the people of
Israel, and that gift was that they would know His true
name.

To the people that did not know His name, it could be
argued that there was an even deeper level of
commitment to Him. To the Native Americans, the
unknown name of the Great Spirit was the greatest test of
faith. All tribes paid respects to God through their
knowing Him without knowing His name. It was put into
their hearts from the very beginning to simply believe, to
have faith, and to know that God existed.

A quote I always liked, quoted by a Dwamish Indian
Tribal member named Seattle, reads as, "Our religion is
the traditions of our ancestors-the dreams of our old men,
given to them in the solemn hours of night by the Great
Spirit; and the visions of our sacred medicine men, and is
written in the hearts of our people." Seattle's words
spoke to me when he said the visions were written in the
hearts of his people. This was the way that I had believed
for many years when it came to understanding God, the
Word, and being His living temple. To have Him
imprinted in my heart, in my life, and in my very being
was my very purpose.

Being a worshiper of God, I always attempted to let
Him lead me as He saw fit. During church services, I
would often pray and ask God to let His power flow and
come throughout the building, and to be able to do

whatever He felt was being needed at that time for His people. I sang, but I also prayed.

Though words would flow out of my mouth, I would always try to find a quiet place inside of my mind over the music being played and the voices being sung. I was attempting to listen to the voice of God, to hear even a small whisper that He was there in the service moving among the people. What was unique however was the fact that when I prayed my prayers, it was not a voice I would hear, but an invisible presence.

The presence that I felt was like a warm rush that would come over me, like the feeling of warm water touching the skin. Then, there was a sense of peace that swept over me. It was a peace that felt like that moment of relief you would get after having a long day or moment after stress in which you felt heavy or tense was removed. The relief also gave me a sense of rejuvenation and renewing in my body and spirit. I would often feel this feeling in moments not only when I was singing, but simply standing in a church service that had a moment of true worship. What also came with this amazing presence was a feeling like there was a voice in its midst.

This voice that was felt was not a voice in the speaking sense. It was a feeling. It was a feeling of a voice talking, and yet no words were heard. The best way to explain it is to picture when you are asking God for help with something, like you are asking Him a question that you would like an answer. When you ask it, if you are attempting to listen to Him, then there is a feeling like the question has been answered. You may not hear a vocal reply, but you know God heard you because your spirit recognizes something the instant the prayer ended. It's the movement of a future event, and the end result becoming reality for God is setting you up to receive an answer! This was the voice without words I felt when the presence of God was on me. It was His presence in my spirit moving in my heart that I was feeling.

What I am pointing out from all of this is that the presence of God is made evident in all of us. His presence is imprinted in all of His creations, the logo of the manufacturer in a way. To the Native Americans, they understood that the Great Spirit was present in their lives even when they did not know how to address Him. To them it did not matter who the name of the Creator was, merely that they were acknowledging His existence in their lives. To me, my flowing in the spirit during praise and worship, as well as in my daily walk, is always in me 24/7 because God lives inside of me.

I am always walking in the spirit, always listening to Him. My faith is that the knowledge that God is speaking to me is there even when there is no voice to be heard. My future is determined the moment I ask God for something, or to help me with something. My life as a living temple is that of a man who knows God's word not just in mind and knowledge, but in heart and truth.

My flow in the spirit comes from a happy heart that will forever sing for joy the songs of praise and worship that ring out from a heart open to the One who lives inside of me. I encourage everyone to learn to open your heart to God by knowing the imprint of God on your heart.

When you know His presence is there simply because He is your creator, then you can hear the words of God as they come over you as a voice of covering. Learn to listen to the voice of God without hearing. Learn to listen to it with your heart, and learn to feel it by His presence washing over you.

Chapter Six

Harmonic Frequencies
or Just Plain Harmony

Colossians 3:16, *"Let the word of Christ dwell in you richly, teaching and admonishing one another in all wisdom, singing psalms and hymns and spiritual songs, with thankfulness in your hearts to God."* It is in our hearts that we are to carry the songs of praise and worship to God. As His spirit is imprinted in the believer's heart, we then are able to create a sound that is unique to the individual who holds it in him.

Each person is created with a unique relationship between them and God. It is a harmony between creation and creator that is special to God. Each life created that finds God, and fellowships with God is a joy to God for it is a one of a kind relationship. Psalm 139:13-16 (a personal favorite) states, *"For you formed my inward parts; you knitted me together in my mother's womb. I praise you, for I am fearfully and wonderfully made. Wonderful are your works; my soul knows it very well. My frame was not hidden from you, when I was being made in secret, intricately woven in the depths of the earth. Your eyes saw my unformed substance; in your book were written, every one of them, the days that were formed for me, when as yet there was none of them."*

God is most pleased when He is in relationship with His creation. Psalm 100:3 states, *"Know that the Lord, He is God! It is He who made us, and we are His; we are His people, and the sheep of His pasture."* It could very well be the one thing that brings Him the most joy in life, just as a father has his most joy when he is in relations with his children.

There is a science that goes with this truth. It is the science of frequency between the spiritual and the physical. In another definition, it is the relationship of the cosmological plain with the physical plain, the relationship of God and man.

It is said that music is a universal language. It is a calculating phenomena of sounds and frequencies that is always in a constant motion. When you listen to the world around you, beats and rhythm can always be heard. When one sound stops, another begins. Whether the noises are as loud as a busy freeway during rush hour traffic, or a semi-quiet night with simple quiet sounds, the natural world is always creating a musical rhythm. One could even say that complete silence has a rhythm to it as silence is a constant single movement of pure quiet. All life has a motion to it that resonates on all sorts of frequencies.

Job 26:10 gives us an interesting scripture. It reads, *"He has inscribed a circle on the face of the waters at the boundary between light and darkness."* There is a boundary between all things that God has created. All life resonates with its own life force, its own harmonic frequency. Even nonliving things such as truth and lies, good and bad, courage and fear all have a separate function that they operate in according to their specific purpose. While separate from each other, it does not mean that they do not interact with each other.

A harmonic, which is known as a wave of a component frequency, are resonated off of time-varying signals. If we were to look at notes played on a piano, each note would have one different sound to it that resonated with a different frequency based off that note. When played in sync or at the same time with another note on a different key or scale, the end result would be a unity of the notes played together in harmony. They create beautiful sounds based off of a unified harmony of different but equal properties.

When dealing with things operating in unity, especially when it involves God, there is a definite power that resonates with it. One voice with God can be a majority, so then imagine what an entire congregation can be like when singing in one accord. This goes back to creating an atmosphere of almost limitless possibilities in a true moment of God's flowing spirit in praise and worship. A unified voice in one accord is perhaps one of the most powerful forces that God has ever created.

We get an example of this in the Old Testament in the book of Genesis 11:6 regarding the Tower of Babel. The scripture reads as, *"And the Lord said, Behold, the people are one, and they have all one language; and this they begin to do: and now nothing will be restrained from them, which they have imagined to do."* It is here that God Himself is admitting that when people come together as one, with one voice, then nothing they do will be impossible to them.

While it is true that the people of the Tower of Babel (believed today to be the Seven Story Ziggurat located in ancient Babylon) were not operating in an atmosphere that was of God (which resulted in their one language becoming mixed and leaving the people to scatter), it was the manner in which they came together in one accord that is relevant. These people of Babel came together as one in one voice, and God Himself knew that because of their unity that nothing was impossible to them. It needs to be noted that it was not the people operating as one that caused God to confuse their languages and scatter them abroad (as seen in Genesis 11:7-8), but the manner in which they were operating in that caused God to do it.

Their unity was in the sense of doing things in a negative manner. Operating in a negative manner would have led them to a dangerous end with disastrous results. This was the reason that God interjected and changed them from one to many peoples.

The Tower of Babel is an example of people not only coming together as one voice, but operating in an atmosphere of harmonic frequency that allows for the flow of harmony produced from the voices of the people, sounds heard, or music played. The unity of different frequencies produced with music is a universal language. All things anywhere and everywhere can be connected through music.

The Greek philosopher Plato, a genius both in philosophy and in science, came to a conclusion that based on the musico-arithmetic structure of an octave, that the world, the human, the universe, and the soul are all connected through the use of music and mathematics. His theory was conceived through the belief that the invisible qualities of the supernatural and the visible qualities of the natural world could come together at a moment where sound was unified to the point that they became connected. As music is a universal language, so to then is mathematics.

The use of mathematics in league with music is done based on the fact that music has qualities that relate to mathematics. Music is calculating, has different levels of frequency, scales, and octaves based on low or high settings that can be added or subtracted too, multiplied or divided from. In Ancient Greece, the brotherhood of the Pythagoreans (followers of Pythagoras, Greek philosopher and mathematician) devoted themselves and their studies to understanding the arithmetic basis of music that was apparent in their studies of mathematics.

As a lover and student of science, I have always attempted to understand the intricacies of God's great creation through the pursuit of knowledge and wisdom. As a musician, I began to study music as a science, or more specifically, I studied the use of sound and its influence on the world around me. I remember one time in my mother's We Who Worship Gathering about two years ago when she had the people in the room all sang together. When the voices sing together in unison, I immediately felt a change in the room and in the atmosphere. The feeling of the room felt comforting, and refreshing in the plainest sense of explanation. Unlike previous mention of God's voice feeling like a covering over the body during a moment of pure worship in church, this feeling was based off of an atmosphere of His presence and dwelling place.

In that moment, you really could feel a glimpse of God's comforting spirit, and His renewing strength of both the mind and body. This feeling is relatable to the scripture of Isaiah 40:23, *"It is He who sits above the circle of the earth, and its inhabitants are like grasshoppers; who stretches out the heavens like a curtain, and spreads them like a tent to dwell in . . ."*

It was from this demonstration that my mother did in the service, and this revelation in the scriptures that I began to experiment with different sounds and different music of praise and worship (separate experiments each) in order to see the interactions with God and the spirit.

Once, I conducted an experiment with a formula using three different sets of praise and worship music on three different computers set in the perimeter of a triangle. The purpose of the triangle was to create a wall of sound directed at me while standing within the triangle as a way to make a wall of praise, and then a wall of worship. My experiment had three points of contact that were used for the test.

The first was to use three different praise songs that were different songs, but with similar melodies to them to bring about a similar rhythm and harmony to them. The second was to use one worship song that was the same worship song played together at the same time in order to produce a constant united vocal and instrumental harmony to it. The third and final part was that the computers were to be placed at different heights, one at a low, medium, and shoulder to head height. The purpose of this last point of contact was to enrapture the whole body in the sounds that were being produced. This was done to see if there was a difference when played at levels of different heights as opposed to played at the same levels of height.

When I played the praise music, I stood right in the middle of the triangle. As the music played, I remained quiet in the middle. Occasionally I would move around in the triangle, sometimes trying to sing and pray a little. I was quiet though, in my mind and in my spirit. I was trying to listen to the worship, to let it flow around me and into me. As I did, something did indeed happen. With the praise music, I felt refreshed. I had worked a bit the morning before I conducted the experiment and was a little tired, but when I played the music about two to three times, I felt as refreshed and rested as if I had just woken up from an eight hour rest.

When I played the worship music, the feeling was quite different. This time with the music, I did feel rested, but also calm, collected, and very peaceful. I had discovered that because I was trying to walk in an atmosphere of praise and worship that I had created a barrier of spiritual sound.

I chose to play two different sets of music for my experiment. For the praise part, I used Native American Christian praise songs. They were all of different songs and tribes, but they flowed well together when played in unison. For the worship, I used the Lord's Prayer sang in Hebrew. Both times the music was perfect for the experiment as it made the atmosphere come alive with the desired outcome. I can honestly say that though any song that is made for God can be used, that there are certain songs and genres that can produce a different outcome based on how the music is used in conjunction with the spirit.

After the tests were concluded, I realized the transformation that I had felt with my body and the spirit were reminiscent of three scriptures that I had read in the Old and New Testaments. First in Philippians 3:21, *"Who will transform our lowly body to be like His glorious body, by the power that enables Him to subject all things to Himself."* In Isaiah 26:3, *"You keep him in perfect peace whose mind is stayed on You, because he trusts in You."* In Proverbs 1:33, *"But whoever listens to me will dwell secure and will be at ease, without dread or disaster."*

The use of sound and music in league with life is the end result of a belief that all life is dependent on harmony. As mentioned earlier, the Greek philosopher Plato believed that music was involved in the structure of the universe. He also believed that it had a direct impact on the soul.

There was a belief in terms of music, the soul, and the universe that there are three kinds of music. Named in Latin, the three were the musica instrumentalis (instrumental music) that was the precise mathematical music of voice and instruments. The musica humana (human music), that was the true physiologically and aesthetically truest music of the human organism in its simplest form. The musica mundane (world music or of world music) that was the entirety of mystical music of the universe in the physical form. These three types of music make up what is known as musica universalis (universal music), or the music of the spheres.

The conclusion to this study is that the universe is bound together by harmony. The harmonic frequencies that resonate off of all life produce those frequencies and work together in unity with all things. When in league with God, the sounds used, the music played, and the frequencies created make for the joining of the supernatural and the natural worlds. It could be argued that the impact the spirit of God has on the human body is almost (or completely) what the human body was like with God before the separation of God and man by sin.

The human body was one with God, unique in relation to the creator and operated in unity with Him and all that surrounded man. Though only a theory, we see some possibility of this belief in Hebrews 4:12, *"For the word of God is living and active, sharper than any two-edged sword, piercing to the division of soul and of spirit, of joints and of marrow, and discerning the thoughts and intentions of heart."* In Galatians 3:28, *"There is neither Jew nor Greek, there is neither slave nor free, there is no male or female, for you are all one in Christ Jesus."*

With God, when we come together in voice, obedience, and unity, we become so much more because we grasp the higher capabilities of the completed man that God intended for us to be with Him. Romans 8:37-39 states, *"No, in all these things we are more than conquerors through Him who loved us. For I am sure that neither death nor life, nor angels nor rulers, nor things present nor things to come, nor powers, nor height nor depth, nor anything else in all creation will be able to separate us from the love of God in Christ Jesus our Lord."*

When we walk with God, then we become more than conquerors.   When we come to Him in praise and worship, then we become complete in Him. Our greatest harmony is seen most when we come together with God

Chapter Seven

Songs of Praise from the Wilderness to the Temple

The body of the church today has a structure and flow of what to do during a church service. Most churches begin with a time of praise and worship to God in order to get the flow of the spirit and the atmosphere right for the flow of God to the people. This is one of the foundational practices of the church seen throughout most of the history of the modern and ancient churches. The beginnings of praise and worship are actually seen as far back as the time of the tabernacle of God in the wilderness during the days of the Israelites 40 year wandering.

In the beginning days of Israel as a free people from Egypt, Moses created a house of dwelling for God and His ark of the covenant. This house would be the tabernacle. The word tabernacle, called Mishkan in Hebrew, means a residence or dwelling place in translation. It was to be a portable dwelling place for the Lord God during the Hebrews time in the wilderness before and after the 40 years wandering.

In Exodus 25:1-2, and follow up verses 25:8-9 the Lord says to Moses, *"And the Lord spoke unto Moses, saying, Speak unto the children of Israel, that they bring Me an offering: of every man that gives it willingly with his heart ye shall take my offering... And let them make Me a sanctuary, so that I may dwell among them. According to all that I show thee, after the pattern of the tabernacle, and the pattern of all the furnishings thereof, even so shall ye make it."* The specifics of the tabernacle are listed in Exodus 26:1-37, and the details of its specifications are not only vast but also vital as the rules for the tabernacle were what determined the outcome of life or death for individuals in the tabernacle (and later the temple). This can be further explained in the details laid out in the Bible's fifty chapters on the tabernacle.

The Jewish people today practice a particular ritual before they enter into their synagogues. They practice this rite of passage into the synagogue before they proceed in so as to get ready for their time of worship to God. This Jewish custom is called Mah Tovu (sometimes pronounced Ma Tovu without the h at the end), which means, "O How Good." This was a prayer that was to be spoken before any of the Jewish congregation wished to enter into the Synagogue to begin their time of worship. Interesting how they performed this prayer in a building that was a resemblance to the ancient tabernacle as synagogues are modeled after the tabernacle of the Old Testament. This shows just how sacred worship is to the Jewish people in league with Yaweh, or YHWH as it is spelled in tradition and respect to the name of God. There are no vowels to make sure all understood His name was so holy, too holy to speak causally.

The tabernacle is referred to with two different names. The first name is the tent of meeting used during the time of Moses, and later as the tent of worship during the time of King David. The tabernacle was the resting place of God during the Israelites time in the wilderness, as well as during their early years in the country of Israel.

It should be noted that while anyone is welcome to worship the Lord God, the tabernacle did have rules and safety precautions that had to be implemented so as only certain people were allowed access to it. Such areas like the Holy of Holies where the ark of the covenant was kept had very specific rules and rituals to be carried out before entering into it.

The Holy of Holies was the most sacred place within the tabernacle. This was where the ark of the covenant, the resting place of the ten commandments, Aaron's budding rod, and a golden jar of mannah (a type of bread from heaven that was manifested on the ground for the Israelites to eat during their time in the wilderness when food was scarce) was placed. The Holy of Holies also housed the mercy seat, the place of communication between God and man, which was located on top of the ark. This was where God would talk and give His instructions to one or two people which would be the only ones allowed to see the ark and the mercy seat.

These two people would be Moses during his lifetime, and the high priest that was selected to come before it to offer sacrifices and hear from the voice of God. After Moses death, the only person permitted to come before the mercy seat would be the high priest, and that honor was highly ritualized.

The high priest was to be the one who was given the responsibility and honor to offer sacrifice to God, as well as worship God before the mercy seat. He was the only one allowed into the Holy of Holies as instructed in Leviticus 16:17, *"No one is allowed inside the tabernacle while Aaron (Moses brother and first high priest of the tribe of the Levites) goes in to make atonement for the most holy place. No One may enter until he comes out again after making atonement for himself, his family, and all the Israelites."* This was a law laid out for the Day of Atonement, and was to be done only once every year on the Day of Atonement. This custom of solo entry for the high priest was essential for the process of entering and leaving the Holy of Holies to the point of life or death depending on how the proper precautions were taken.

The ritual practices for the Day of Atonement, as well as for the sacrifices that were to be made had to be exact. It says so specifically in Leviticus 16:13, *"If he follows these instructions, he will not die."* When Aaron and future high priests would enter into the Holy of Holies for the sacrifices and worship of the Lord both in the tabernacle and Solomon's temple, the priest was to be very careful about entering into the room of the Lord's presence. While not to go into too much detail, one interesting note was that whenever a priest would enter into the Holy of Holies, they would have a rope wrapped around their waist. If the priest were to die, then the other priests were simply to pull him out of the Holy of Holies via the rope and not set foot in the Holy of Holies.

It has to be understood that the tabernacle and the temple are early representations of the body of Christ. Furthermore, the tabernacle and temple were the resting places of the spirit of God during His time of dwelling among the people of Israel. The very presence itself can be so great that it could overwhelm and kill anyone in His presence if someone did not tread the presence carefully. Moses could not stand in the presence of God for fear of being killed by His glory while receiving the ten commandments. The Apostle Paul was blinded while looking directly at the presence of God on the road to Damascus.

The Day of Atonement is just one of the many sacred days and years that were laid out for the Israelites to honor and worship God. Other days that can be mentioned are the Festival of Trumpets in which they would sound long trumpet blasts before the Day of Atonement, and then the Year of Jubilee in which is the 50th year of seven years of Sabbath accumulated to which loud trumpet blasts are sounded to declare a time of jubilee for the year that marks a time of restoration of all that was returned to the Israelites. These days are significant for they are done with instruction to use musical instruments to ring in times of celebration, rest, and atonement in the name of the Lord, to honor Him, and bring restoration and rest to the Lord's holy people. These days are laid out with instruction in Leviticus 23:23-25 for the Festival of Trumpets, and 25:8-23 for the Year of Jubilee.

The instructions in Leviticus were laid out during the time of Moses and the first years of the tribe of the Levites as the appointed high priests for God and the tabernacle. During the time of Moses, he referred to the tabernacle as the tent of meeting in which the people would meet with God. After David became King David of Israel, he would move the tabernacle again (the last time before his son, King Solomon, would build the temple of God). When King David would set up the tabernacle during his reign though, he would call the tabernacle the tent of worship.

In Acts 13:22 God says that, *"I have found in David the son of Jesse a man after My heart, who will do all My will."* David was a man who deeply loved God. His love of God was so great that even when he committed acts of sin, though God would punish him, He would also give mercy and forgiveness to David unlike any who came before him. It was for this reason that perhaps God chose to make David's lineage that from which Jesus would be born and establish the kingship and priesthood when the time came for the Son of man to be born.

We read in II Samuel 6 that David brought the ark of the covenant to the city of Jerusalem. Throughout the entire chapter we read that the whole time the ark was being moved that the whole of Israel was celebrating its arrival, *"with all their might, singing songs and playing all kinds of musical instruments"* as quoted in verse I Chronicles 13:8. After a brief stay at the house of a man named Obed-Edom, David finally brought the ark to the city of Jerusalem.

When the ark was coming into the city, David had the men carrying the ark stop so he could make a sacrifice before it. After killing a fattened calf and ox, David then danced before the ark wearing a priest's tunic and praised God with all his might. As he did this to honor God, the rest of the people also brought the ark up to the city with great shouts of praise and great trumpet blowing.

In the book of I Chronicles, we read that David began to establish a new approach to the rules and protocols of the tabernacle. The book of I Chronicles gives detailed information to the structured order that David used in order to bring the ark into the city, how the priests were established, what songs and instruments were to be used in its approach, and which priests and tribes were to be given the responsibility for the praises that were to be used in the transportation of the ark to the city. In the beginning of chapter 22, David begins to prepare not just the tabernacle for the ark of the covenant but also the building of a temple for God.

In the 23rd chapter of I Chronicles, David begins to setup the work of the Levites in the work of worship in the temple. He begins by giving them instruments of worship that he had made. David sets the Levites up to begin several duties for the temple, but one of the most important duties is the establishment of the praise and worship before God. In I Chronicles 23:30 we read, *"And each morning and evening they stood before the Lord to sing songs of thanks and praise to Him."* This duty of praise and worship was to be carried out, mentioned in I Chronicles 23:5, by 4,000 Levites equipped with the instruments of praise that David had made. Can you imagine 4,000 people charged with the duty and responsibility to sing songs morning and evening to God? More astounding is that this time of praise morning and evening was not to be done simply in the hours of the morning and evening, but at all times in between morning and evening. In I Chronicles 23:31 it reads that that all the appointed numbers of the Levites served in the Lord's presence, *"at all times, following all the procedures they had been given,"* and never stopping for anything, not even once.

In I Chronicles 25 David and his military commanders began to proclaim God's messages through the use of music accompaniment from a harp, lyres, and cymbals. I Chronicles 6:8 reads, *"All these men were under the direction of their fathers as they made music at the house of the Lord. Their responsibilities included the playing of cymbals, lyres, and harps at the house of God. Asaph, Jeduthun, and Heman reported directly to the king. They and their families were all trained in making music before the Lord, and each of them-288 in all-was an accomplished musician. The musicians were appointed to their particular term of service by means of sacred lots, without regard to whether they were young or old, teacher or student."* This means that all the musicians who were to play in God's house were trained and educated to play music. They were musicians who were dedicated and selected to perform a sacred duty to God regardless of who they were, or what their status was. The position of the one to play music was so important that only a person of great skill was to be appointed to play the music of God during their 24 hour service time.

From the wilderness of Canaan to the metropolis of Jerusalem, we see that the history of praise and worship in the tabernacle carried an atmosphere of major change to it. From a tent of meeting in the days of Moses, to a tent of worship in the time of David we see a huge rise in the use of music and song in the house of God. It could be theorized that to David, there was something that was unique inside of him that made him see the use of music in league with God differently than those that approached God with standard methods of sacrifice and worship used in the older rituals of the tabernacle. Perhaps it was due to his time as a shepherd tending his father Jesse's flocks.

As a young man out in the wild, alone, and possibly sometimes for days at a time, David would have time to ponder on things. We know that he wrote his own songs of praise while he was a shepherd, and that his music was known well enough to have him come and play before King Saul himself. It might be possible that David listened in the quiet of the wilderness to see if he could hear the voice of God, or at least feel the spirit of God, that Moses and Joshua felt when they went to be alone with God in the wilderness. Even if God did not speak directly to David, it is possible that the sheer wonder of dwelling on God inspired David to write his music and poetry.

It was the attempt to listen to the spirit, to reach out with his faith, to look up at a night sky filled with stars and see God's great creation that drove David's inspiration to write works of beauty reserved only for the Lord of hosts. Whatever the reason that inspired David, it is obvious that it gave him the skill and desire to sing songs of praise first in the quiet of the sheepfold, then in the presence of the king, and finally in the presence of the King of Kings.

Before he died, David made one final prayer of praise to God. In I Chronicles 29:11, a small part of the prayer reads:

"Yours, O Lord, is the greatness, the power, the glory, the victory, and the majesty. Everything in the heavens and on earth is yours, O Lord, and this is your kingdom. We adore You as the one who is over all things. Riches and honor come from You alone, for You rule over everything. Power and might are in Your hand, and it is at your discretion that people are made great and given strength."

It is with this that David could best be described as the man who started temple praise and worship.

Chapter Eight

Praise and Worship and Principles of War

The use of praise and worship is a powerful tool to bring about change in the atmosphere. They can be great tools of warfare that are available to the believer who uses them. While many believers, teachings, and books have often spoken of a Christian as an individual of peace based on the teachings of Christ being defined as principles of peace and turning the other cheek, this view of Jesus' teaching is not the whole truth of what Christ was instructing us on. The Bible is full of teachings on peace, but also on warfare. Ecclesiastes 3:8 reads, *"A time to love, and a time to hate; a time for war, and a time for peace."*

Jesus Christ is a man of war in many ways. While He is the prince of Peace, Jesus has been described in many scriptures as a conqueror and fighter. The Hebrew definition of peace is, "To destroy the stronghold that establishes chaos." Jesus is our Prince of Peace. He as "Peace" has destroyed the stronghold that tried to establish chaos, namely fallen Lucifer, now Satan. In Revelation 17:14 we read, *"They will make war on the Lamb, and the Lamb will conquer them, for He is Lord of Lords and King of Kings, and those with Him are called chosen and faithful."* We are commanded in II Timothy 2:3 to, *"Share in suffering as a good soldier of Christ Jesus."*

While we wage war not with weapons in the natural, we do wage war in the spirit. Ephesians 6:12 tells us, *"For we do not wrestle against flesh and blood, but against the rulers, against the authorities, against the cosmic powers over this present darkness, against the spiritual forces of evil in the heavenly places."* Because we wage war in the spirit, we also wage war in the natural realm as what we fight against takes footholds against us both in the spirit and the natural world.

The power of praise and worship is a tool of war. King David was a great warrior who wrote songs of praise both for war and peace. Joshua, the second judge of Israel after Moses, was a warrior of God who used priests, trumpets, and the cry of the people to bring the walls of Jericho down at the command of God and His angelic commanders. The songs of praise and worship aided Paul and Silas as they sang songs that caused the prison they were in to come open, their chains to fall, and bring the prison guard who was watching them to God all in the same night. These men made evident that praise and worship are tools for war, tools for bringing down walls, and to set people free from bondage.

We begin to wage war in the natural realm through our songs of praise and worship. Individually and together, praise and worship trigger the changes that open up the realm of the spirit to begin setting up our methods of war. In today's age of music, the world has many new forms of music which can result in very positive or negative reactions with the people who listen to them. Two unique styles today that have a very powerful following would be that of the music of rap and hip hop.

The influence of rap and hip hop has been unique as it is one of the few music styles to use a sense of 'pure life expression' in its lyrics and style of music. Rap is based off of the events that have often transpired in the rappers life, or uses particular themes that they feel is something they can put their passions into when they sing and speak about it. The lyrics and power in the words spoken can be quite deep and soul piercing. There influence can either be very positive or very negative.

One main theme in rap is that of the individual's struggle, pain, or tragedy and the rapper uses much of his personal convictions. The words will often carry a side that impacts the spirit of the person listening. In modern American history, negative rap and hip hop have had a troubling twist on the people who have listened to them. Many individual artists who were young and in their prime met with unfortunate endings from being murdered, imprisoned for criminal activity. Others have become paranoid and committed suicide. This negative side though reveals something. If the negative side of rap and hip hop can have such a profound impact on people, whether the singer or the hearer, then the potential of the positive impacts of rap and hip hop on people could also be powerful.

Christian music artists today have made great strides in the music of rap and hip hop. There has been an impact in the Christian youth today with the interactions of rap and hip hop as many young artists are releasing out songs and performances that send a clear and positive message to its viewers. Many churches have Christian rap groups that perform for their churches. They are usually all revolving around a particular theme of God that brings what they are trying to say together in one voice. It brings a different side out when you hear a positive message in the voices of the rappers speaking and singing.

As a musician, I enjoy rap and hip hop music. Learning to understand the intricacies of sound and music in league with the body, I have discovered that rap music has very deep levels. I say this based on two things that I have come to understand when it comes to rap. Those two things are impact and emotion.

The emotions in the songs can have multiple sides to them. In secular kinds of rap, the types of songs have a theme of crime, drugs, sex, and other negative stereotypes to them. These topics often bring about emotions of hate, anger, rage, prejudice, and other negative emotions that resonate within the songs. The listener would then have these emotions fed to them, and if not careful will allow the negativity to take hold or take root in them. This manifestation of impartation that is of the flesh that we listen to is rooted in the warnings of Galatians 6:7-8, *"Do not be deceived: God is not mocked, for whatever one sows, that will he also reap. For the one who sows to his own flesh will from the flesh reap corruption, but the one who sows to the spirit will from the spirit reap eternal life."*

While there is a bad side to rap and hip hop, like a coin with two sides, there is a good side to it. Rap and hip hop that portrays a positive image can be just as powerful, if not more, than the negative rap that is often heard. As the previous scripture in Galatians reads, those who sow things from the spirit will reap eternal life from it. What is the spirit in its purest form? In its root basics, the spirit is a constant source of positive energy. All good and righteous things are from God, and the spirit is of God. The spirit not only produces happiness and joy, but also produces works within a person that are positive and encouraging. The Spirit will give the one who is willing to walk in it an eye and ear to hear and see all the things that are wrong in the world, the things that corrupt and distort it.

There are three scriptures that describe the interactions of the world and man and what we could describe as the impact of negative rap on mankind. These scriptures are Ephesians 2:2, Ephesians 5:11, and II Corinthians 4:4. One theme of rap today is that of disobedience. This disobedience can be in the form of disobedience to the law, to authority such as parental or civil, to words of wisdom, and anything else that you could defy or stand against. This is described within Ephesians 2:2, *"In which you once walked, following the course of this world, following the prince of the power of the air, the spirit that is now at work in the sons of disobedience."*

Another theme in negative rap is one of anti-righteousness. This means the unfruitful works of the world such as doing drugs, drinking, smoking, breaking the law, and other things that we understand to be wrong and evil are released through the sound waves and words of negative, anti-righteousness. Ephesians 5:11 says, *"Take no part in the unfruitful works of darkness, but instead expose them."* The disobedience that is mentioned in negative rap will promote the desire to commit the unfruitful works of darkness as both go hand in hand.

All negative rap has one underlying message that many people don't realize. It is the message of conformity. It is the message of conforming to the same image of an individual that is to be against God or anything promoting good intentions. All the negativity produced in rap puts into the mind of a person an image of an outlaw, a thief, a man that has to become something other than what is good and positive in order to get ahead in life. It is true that some rappers have become famous and rich from this kind of music. But, many rich and famous rappers that are known have often met with the same ending of death, imprisonment, or a life of constant hardship depending on what they have sown to bring it about. II Corinthians 4:4 reads, *"In their case the god of this world has blinded the minds of the unbelievers, to keep them from seeing the light of the gospel of the glory of Christ, who is the image of God."*

People never realize that God Himself was a type of outlaw. His whole time on the earth was that of a man who went against the establishment, who promoted individuality against the image of His day. Christ wanted people to have their own unique walk with God that promoted them to a higher level within themselves, their relationship with God, and their prosperity in life. The images of this world have blinded people to this realization that it's not in the negative, but in the positive flowing of God (or anything positive for that matter) great things can be accomplished. Positive produces positive, so even if a person does not know God but they choose to be positive, their life will produce positive fruit.

The flow of the world image of rap and hip hop have done exactly what most fans of rap and hip hop didn't expect. They have taken on the image of everyone else, the image of the same person, the image of conformity. It's this kind of image that not only is the same one that those on their way to hell take on, but also of the image that just makes life never changing and always the same thing over and over again. Negative produces negative.

When we walk in the positive flow of God, then we walk a path that is far different than the negative path of this world. Psalm 37:4 reads, *"Delight yourself in the Lord, and He will give you the desires of your heart."* God has the desire to give us our desires. This simple scripture in Psalms gives perfect testament to how God gives us what we want. Our desires are unique from everyone else, and that goes against an image of conformity.

God never intended for people to be the same. All are equal in the sight of God as human beings, but all are uniquely different from each other as they are a unique creation in God. People are people, animals are animals, plants are plants, but none are ever the same as another.

When we discuss equality in the United States, we understand "equality for all" but must realize that simply means everyone is entitled to the same rights and privileges that all seek in the United States. The individual American citizen makes his or her own path in life. Even a soldier in the United States military, a symbol of brotherhood and equality among each soldier, joins up for their own unique and personal reasons (college, career, etc.). Because the United States is a nation founded under God, we then realize that while equal, we are to make our own unique path in a nation founded just for that purpose. In God uniqueness is celebrated. The only conformity is to submit to God's highest will and purpose for each one of us.

When we listen to Christian rap and hip hop, there is a flow to it that is different than other kinds of music. In a sense, rap and hip hop are forms of 'life music.' This means that the music that is performed is alive, giving off a feeling of who the person performing it is feeling. Indeed, the atmosphere that is emulated from a rap concert is one that is alive with the spirit of the person performing it. It is more from the soul transformed by the spirit of God.

We can understand this as one soul with God is a majority. The soul of a person is a host among itself. Jesus says in Luke 15:7, *"Just so, I tell you, there will be more joy in heaven over one sinner who repents than over ninety-nine righteous persons who need no repentance."* Those with something to say, those who confess, repent, relent, and speak from their heart can impact an entire population. A single soul can change an entire nation in less than 24 hours because of the words and their testimony.

During the days of the Chaldean Empire of ancient Babylonia, and the capitol city of Babylon, King

Nebuchadnezzar had three such souls in his kingdom. The wise men of his court, Shadrach, Meshach, and Abednego were men of God who lived only for God. When the king had grown too arrogant in his ways and tried to turn himself into a god, these three men stood against him. Choosing to obey God above their king, Nebuchadnezzar decided to kill them. While he failed to kill them as God Himself prevented them from being burned to death in a fiery furnace (the story of the image of Nebuchadnezzar and the fiery furnace can be read in the book of Daniel), the king realized that these men were a threat to his rule.

Three simple men who were willing to choose God over their kings own ruler was a threat that would cause Babylon to turn upside down. When a soul has something inside of it that brings conviction, it can change a person. When it is endowed with the spirit of God, it can make things shake and tremble. Those who walk in testimony with the spirit of God in their lives can break down nations, and cause radical changes in a very short period of time.

Rap and hip hop have this type of edge to them when they are played before the masses. When performed together with the spirit of God, the impact on the listeners can be profound. The words that are spoken in rap are often words of deep emotional drama that people listen to because they want to take something away from it.

When you take an event in your life and you speak about it with conviction putting your heart and soul into it, then you can change a person. There are two types of changes that a person will experience when they change their nature. These changes are a head change followed by a heart change.

When words spoken are heard by the listener, the sounds go to the head of a person. Then that is where you see change in the mind of a person which is a head change. It's in the next level of heart change, where, the real work takes place in a person. You can plant the root of a heart change inside of a head change, but it has to be planted deep. Proverbs 23:7 says, "*As a person thinks so is he.*"

A heart change is the hardest thing for a person to do because it is a life changing event. An example of this is when you give your heart to God. It takes a confession of faith to bring the salvation of God, but it begins when you really consider what you are doing. When you believe the word in your mind, then you must believe it in your heart. You hear the Word spoken with your brain, but you must accept it in your heart. Faith is knowing that the word is real, and when you come to know the word of God in your mind and heart together, then that is when you know for sure that you are saved. That is when the real life change can begin. Change starts with knowing!

To speak or sing as a true believer is to bring a conviction inside of you that makes your words so much more impacting. You take on this persona of a person who speaks the way they believe, and who walks they way they feel. That is called living a godly lifestyle. When we can apply our godly lifestyle to the influence of rap and hip hop, we can then create music with a powerful message.

The use of rap and hip hop today can be great instruments of war due to their soul impacting music style. The simple fact that they can have an impact in a positive or negative way so profoundly on individuals is a demonstration of just how powerful a tool it is. In the right hands, it can be one of the most powerful tools available to the believer in singing praise and worship to God, and for waging war in the name of God.

There is no doubt that the Christian of today has to begin operating in a mindset of war. The world today is drastically changing every day, and we have no idea whether its turn is going to be good or bad. We have to begin to learn how to use praise and worship to wage war in the spirit, how to listen to God's principles of war, and how to adapt it to the natural world. When we can start to operate in this style, we begin to work in the same way that the prophets, judges, and warriors of God from the days of the Old and New Testament operated in it.

Out of all the members of my family that have sung and worshiped God, the one that I would say was the beginning to understanding how to wage war in the spirit would have to be my sister. Gabrielle Christian Salem was one of the greatest people that I will ever know. Though quite young, her impact in my life taught me things that when I dwell on them now, I realize they were what I needed to learn in order to grow up within myself.

My sister is a strong Christian, but more than that she is a wonderful human being. She had a gift to make people smile because she enjoyed seeing people happy. She could make a person understand that they were special even when they did not think they were. Her gifts in music were quite amazing for someone only in her early years of life. She had a very developed voice and ability to remember lyrics to songs when she sang and performed for people. She never appeared embarrassed or scared whenever she got up on stage or TV to sing in front of God and people. She really appeared to enjoy what she was doing. Despite her age, she could be said to take great pride in her singing and worship of God.

By the time she was 5, my sister was diagnosed with a brain tumor. This was without a doubt the hardest thing that my family would ever have to go through. For the longest time, my family and friends did everything they could to get Gabrielle healed. Having been told that she would only have eight weeks to live, my sister's determination to fight what was happening to her beat the doctors diagnosis into the ground. These months with her was the greatest of challenges, but also the greatest prevailing and strengthening of faith in God that we would ever face.

Despite being sick, my sister still would get up and sing in church because it was what she believed needed to be done for God. She still made people laugh and feel happy even when it was hard for her to do much herself. After being bed ridden, whenever people came to see her, Gabrielle would still do things to bring a smile to people's faces. She would put on wigs to make people laugh, draw pictures for them, and have people sit and play dolls or video games with her and just have fun.

Her spirit and outward portrayal of who she was in God and who God was inside of her left such an impression on people whenever they were around her. Even after she went home to be with the Lord my sister's happy spirit still lingered in the atmosphere as those who were close to her always remembered what a joy it was to be around her, and how she just loved life even in the hardest of times.

Gabrielle's example of bringing out the best and positive in people whenever they were around her is an example of what people can feel from someone else who has a certain flow of life in them. If someone feels a flowing of something very positive in their lives, they bring about that feeling in others around them. If it is negative, the same will happen to those that feel the negativity. Music is an expression of the deepness inside of a person. The interactions of music when in league with God are a very deep moving sensation.

We read in James 5:13 that, *"Is anyone among you suffering? Let him pray. Is anyone cheerful? Let him sing praise."* There are two different parts of this scripture. The first part that states if someone is suffering, then they should pray in order to find a solution to their suffering. The second part says if someone is cheerful, then sing praise to show the joy that they are feeling inside.

Prayer is often done in spoken word or in quiet thought to convey a particular message between God and the one praying. Singing is done because you are raising your voice in happiness often at times in front of other people to portray your joy where others can hear you. To sing songs of your cheerfulness is to invite others to join in with you to be cheerful themselves. This is also a way to teach people how to wage war in the spirit, and within them.

Why the need to wage war? First, this is not war in the conventional sense with guns, knives, and physical combat. This sense of war is the war of spirit or spiritual war. However, when we pray in the spirit, or sing in the spirit that affects the spiritual as well as the natural. Our spirit, mind, and body are all connected. I Corinthians 14:15 says, *"What am I to do? I will pray with my spirit, but I will pray with my mind also; I will sing praise with my spirit, but I will sing with my mind also."* This means that what we do spiritually, we can also do naturally.

My mother would often teach me about putting down my flesh and to kill it each day. This refers to me not thinking like a normal man, but as a man who listens to God using wisdom and knowledge in my daily walk. Everything that we do has an impact on us. Ezekiel 28:13 states, *"And they come to you as people come, and they sit before you as my people, and they hear what you say but they will not do it; for with lustful talk in their mouths they act; their heart is set on their gain."*

Our flesh by definition is our natural way of thinking, speaking, and wanting. Our spirit is our godly way of thinking, speaking, and wanting. Both exist within us, but are not on the same page or agreement with each other. Both want different things, and the flesh side is usually going to want things that are not good for us. Because of this, we must train our flesh to operate under our spirit side. We must kill our flesh everyday in order to let God's spirit flow, and to let our better godly existence thrive.

Our flesh is stubborn, and will often put up a fight. Because of this, we must fight our flesh everyday in order to bring it down, to kill it. When we do, then we can operate freely in the spirit and let God's power flow. Romans 8:13 states, *"For if you live according to the flesh you will die, but if by the spirit you put to death the deeds of the body, you will live."* When we realize that we must fight our flesh in order to empower our spirit for God, we must then understand that the world is also like our flesh.

The world will bring things against you, attack you, and try to kill you in one form or another. While the world is not our flesh as it has its own spirit, we must fight against the world in the same way that we fight our own flesh. The world has a flesh spirit on it, and we must kill that flesh spirit if we are to let God's power flow through it. In Romans 8:9, Paul tells the believer, *"You, however, are not in the flesh but in the spirit, if in fact the spirit of God dwells in you. Anyone who does not have the spirit of Christ does not belong to Him."*

The flesh spirit of the world strives to be away from God. The world was created by God, but like all things alive it has a free will to choose. The spirit of the world is that of a sinful nature due to the introduction of sin into God's created world. Because of that, then the nature of the world and God are on opposite sides. The nature of the world and the nature of God cannot coexist. Therefore, we must strive to stay away from the nature of the world and only embrace the nature of God.

Because of the need to resist the nature of the world, we must be willing to wage war against it. We build ourselves up by putting on the armor of God, coming together with the shout of victory, and standing firm against the devil and his minions. This however is only the beginning of what we need to do. We must begin to strive to stir the spirit to begin waging war against all the forces of the enemy, the wicked one, and the world. We can't be lukewarm in our approach to fighting off the forces of the devil. We have to stand, shout, stomp our feet, shake our fists, say, 'Bring it on,' and be prepared to dish it out with God's power backing us up.

Some of the rap and hip hop songs that I have listened to were written by Christian artists that had a very clear message about the Christian man making war. I listened to one artist that spoke clearly about all the things that come against us in the world. When I listened to the lyrics I felt a sense of conviction on how   we live in this world with God in our lives. I realized that too many Christians have only walked or tip-toed their way through this world in their daily lives, and only paid a certain amount of attention of how to really take a stand against those things that bring us down. We should make war, fight, and crush our enemy beneath our feet, and stand tall in what we are in Christ!

Romans 8:36 reads, *"As it is written, "'For your sake we are being killed all the daylong; we are regarded as sheep to be slaughtered."'"* Then in Romans 8:37 it declares, *"No, in all these things we are more than conquerors through Him who loved us."* To the world we may seem as lambs to the slaughter, but that is the worldview of us who love God. We are not lambs, but lions who serve the Lion of Judah! When we are backed into a corner we shouldn't cower in fear, but fight with the fierceness and ferocity that a cornered animal would fight.

Jesus stood His ground in His walk on the earth against the masses that came against Him. He stood the test against Satan in His time of testing in the wilderness. He answered all the questions and criticisms that the Pharisees, Sadducees, and other religious leaders brought against Him. When He saw the temple of God being used for profit and gain instead of for the purposes of God, He made a whip and tore into the money changers, salesmen, and taxmen that made the temple their den of thieves and kicked them all out of His house (we could say Jesus was the first to use the phrase "This is my house" that is so commonly used in the world today). When He died on the cross, He did it with no drugs or tranquilizers which He was offered frequently by the Romans to help ease His pain but refused, and took it all in full stride. Since that was the attitude of Christ while He was on the earth, then that's the attitude we need to take when we know we have to be more than conquerors when times call for it.

Making war in the spirit begins in the use of praise and worship. When we use praise and worship to bring about the presence of the Holy Spirit, then we must begin to declare war in the spirit. .

When I make war in the spirit, I do it based on what circumstances I am facing. Being in a position to do the work of God my family has come under attack after attack due to the work that we have been doing ever since we started Salem Family Ministries. My whole family has felt an attack of the devil from very small things, to life or death situations. Understanding what you need to speak, to profess, to confess, to bring before God, how to speak to Him, and what your attitude towards Him and the spirit is helps you clarify and lay a strategic plan for spiritual warfare.

About five years ago, my mother had just had attack in her colon. As a cancer survivor, my mother gets constant checkups to see the progress of her health, and to check if there are any traces of anything cancerous in her body. During her last check up, the doctors discovered a cancerous polyp in her colon. Doctors were able to remove it, a second surgery and further removal of her colon was required. While the surgery was successful, that was not the end of the battle.

A few days after Mom had returned home, she had a bad feeling in her stomach. Throughout the day she had what appeared to be pain in her stomach that we thought would go away after some rest and medication. It didn't go away that night but got increasingly worse. She had to be taken to the emergency room around 2:00 AM in the morning. Still in pain, the doctors had to ease her pain with medicine to allow her to rest. The whole family spent the night with her in the hospital room. By the next morning everyone was exhausted and stressed and she was no better, but even worse pain.

After being moved to another room in the main part of the hospital, after 2 days the doctors performed a series of tests to see what was going on with her. The doctors discovered that her colon had become twisted and was causing her severe stomach and abdominal problems. They wanted to perform surgery on her to try and untwist her colon. But in truth that did not sit well with me. After seeing her go through one surgery to remove cancer 7 years earlier then, another surgery to remove another cancerous part of her colon, and now hearing talk of a third surgery, within a few days, I said enough was enough.

As I went to her room the night they informed us of her need to have surgery, I was tired and angry. My father had stayed with Mom so my brother and I could go home and get some rest, but I was not rested. I spent time walking alone dwelling on all that had happened. I was fed up with these constant attacks and attempts on the lives of my family. I didn't really know what I could do at this point.

Days before when I heard about my mother needing surgery, I was at college attending class. I had stepped outside and sat down in front of one of the large pillars that propped up the building's roof. I spent several minutes in prayer, and then I began to ponder on things.

I always had faith that whatever I prayed for God would answer. I believed that God would heal my mother as He did before because there was still much work for her to do for Him. When a person is called, God will take care of them. More so because they have such desire to do His will. It wasn't the healing that I pondered on, but the constant attacks by the devil and the world.

I thought about I could fight against these attacks differently than what I had been doing. When things happened, I prayed, had faith, and knew God was in control. Despite all of these things though there was something missing. What was it?

That was the question that had stuck with me from that moment outside of class right up to the moment I had gone back to see Mom the night we were to discuss her surgery. That night, I sat in a chair next to my mother's bed watching her trying to sleep. She was not resting well, and was having pains back and forth since the night we took her to the hospital. When my father thought it was time for us to let her get some sleep, he had us all come together to pray for her before we left. That was when everything began to fall into place for me.

As we began to pray, I didn't know why but I felt different. We each prayed a prayer for her, and when it came my time, I started pleading the blood of Jesus over her as I do in all my prayers. Something stirred in me and my words began to change.

I started to speak against the attack as if I was directly talking to it face to face. I began to command it to come out of my mother that instant, to be removed, to be killed, and never to return to her. I began to speak things I never thought I would say and began to speak to God in a commanding voice. I wasn't commanding God, but I was commanding His healing power to come and do its job.

One part of the prayer I remember speaking was where I said that this woman (Cheryl) had devoted her life to God, did everything that she could to honor and obey Him, sacrificed her body and life to go to places all over the world to do His work, and had a family that was willing to do the same. She had suffered a terrible car crash, had seen her daughter suffer a brain tumor and die, and had fought cancer twice. Now she was facing another attack in her colon, and I was fed up with it.

I commanded the pain to come out of her, and that she never have to face this again. I told God to come right then and there and give this woman of God freedom from this attack. I was taking authority over something that for too long had been a hindrance to her, my family, and to me.

As I prayed, I felt all kinds of emotions coming out of me that had been built up for the longest time. In truth I was angry. This anger stemmed from years of seeing these attacks happen again and again. Finally it was enough. I was not going to let these things of the devil, the world, or anything else that sought to attack us come at us any longer.

I prayed, took authority, confessed my desires, and brought my faith out laying it on the table for God to understand. I needed His healing power right then and there. I wasn't going to settle for anymore curses. Only the full manifestation of God's healing presence was what I would settle accept. After I finished praying, then the physical workings of God healing power began to take place.

Five minutes after I began praying, my mother began to feel different. Getting up from bed, she suddenly bolted to the restroom. She moved so fast that she pulled the IV out of her arm, but still didn't stop moving. Afterwards my mother began to look well again. Her colon had completely untwisted in minutes through the power of Jesus through prayer!

The pains that she was feeling in her twisted colon were instantly gone. Instead of going home, we all stayed and had a doctor come in and examine her. After a quick checkup and examination, then doctor came back in and had a look of amazement on his face. Apparently the twisted colon had untwisted. The doctor then told us that if things progressed at this rate, then my mother would not need surgery and could possibly go home the next day. Sure enough, she was well enough the following day to be released and sent home. We kept an eye on her to make sure everything went well, she was healed!

My mentioning of this miraculous healing is for two reasons. The first is the fact that when this attack happened, I was no longer wanting to operate in the levels of the spirit that I had been in up to that point. When I prayed, I took a different approach to my prayers and to my authority in Jesus name. The second is that when I prayed, then the authority that God gives to each and every one of us took command. I took command of the gifts of the spirit and the healing power of God that is present when you speak for healing. I was no longer praying for the belief in healing, but for the knowing that healing was going to happen. I was bringing the attack to the enemy and the sickness that had manifested in my mother. I didn't just speak to have it removed; I spoke to have it be killed. I waged war against it when I spoke to it. Because of that level of operating in the spirit the colon untwisted. God was able to heal her immediately.

James 1:12 tells us that, *"Blessed is the man who remains steadfast under trial, for when he has stood the test he will receive the crown of life, which God has promised to those who love Him."* I stayed faithful to God in that time of trial and testing. My mother always stayed true to her faith and to her love of God during her times of testing and trial. I honestly believe that I received the crown of life in that moment when I waged war on that foul colon attack that had manifested after the battle of cancer my mother had beaten through Jesus.

What I felt inside of me when I had prayed was not produced by my flesh or physical attributes of mind and body, but by my spirit. The words that stirred within me to speak had been manifested from the need for healing, the craving to grasp it, and to see it in action.

Three scriptures come to mind when understanding what is made in your spirit during trial and testing. The first is in I Thessalonians 5:21, *"But test everything, hold fast what is good."* I held onto my faith and to the belief that she would be healed. I then took the faith of knowing that she would be healed. No longer just simple belief, but the gift of knowing in faith that healing would occur.

The second scripture is in II Timothy 1:13, *"Follow the pattern of the sound words you have heard from me, in faith and love that are in Christ Jesus."* The words that I wanted to speak, and the words that I needed to speak came to me from the spirit. When I prayed for my mother this time, I spoke with conviction in my words. I was not going to stand around any longer and wait. The only kind of waiting I have ever accepted was that of waiting on God. I understood that what we desire is not the same as God's desire, and for that we have to wait upon Him to do what He sees fit at the appropriated moment. I did not have to wait this time though for God put in me what I needed to speak and to command. This was my chance to do what I believed God for, and I did not hesitate.

I took His words, His healing, His principles of war, and I fought the enemy. This then lines up with the 3rd and final scripture from II Thessalonians. In II Thessalonians 2:14, *"To this He called you through our gospel, so that you may obtain the glory of our Lord Jesus Christ."* In that moment of belief, of knowing, and prayer for healing I believe that the glory of God had come full force.

The glory of God is the most powerful force in all of creation. The glory is what had covered mankind before the fall of Adam and Eve in the Garden of Eden. It is a source of constant positive that produces nothing but good results. Only the blood of Jesus, the covering of His blood, is equal to the glory of God. When man fell, Jesus came and died for us to pay for our sin. He gave us a new covering with His own blood to protect us from the negativity of sin. His blood is healing and His glory is healing.

When I pleaded for the blood and spoke the words of healing, then the glory of God and the blood of Jesus came over my mother. They stood against the attack, covered her wounds, and removed all that came against her. This was the end result of my war against the disease. The end result of healing for the renewing of her body and protection from further attack. It also provided rest for all of us. With no need for surgery, my family and I could take time to rest, heal, and praise God for the miracle that He gave us and my mother.

The point of mentioning this miraculous and amazing time in my life is to teach you about two things you need for making war in the spirit. Those two things are authority and command. We must understand that those who serve God have to take authority and command of what is given to them. John 14:26 reads, *"But the Helper, the Holy Spirit, whom the Father will send in My name, He will teach you all things and bring to your remembrance all that I have said to you."* We have the knowledge and understanding given to us by the Holy Spirit. God gives further teaching of authority and command in II Timothy 4:2, *"Preach the word; be ready in season and out of season; reprove, rebuke, and exhort, with complete patience and teaching."*

In the militaries of the United States and Israel today, soldiers are always on constant readiness to go to war. Active duty soldiers, reservists, and auxiliary forces are trained to be activated at the simple ring of a phone.

When a soldier becomes activated for war, they drop everything they are doing, put on their uniform, put on their armor, grab their weapons, and head off to war the minute they are ready to go. Like the soldiers in the natural who are ready 24/7, so too are we as soldiers of Christ to be ready for war. We are to be prepared and ready to take authority and command of any and all situations that come our way.

Since it is in the spirit that we are to declare war, then we must use all the gifts that the spirit gives us to wage war. Our songs, shouts, scriptures, praise, worship, and everything else that brings about the presence of God are to be put towards bringing the principles of war that God has in the waiting for us to use. God is the God of peace, but He is also the God that makes war for on behalf of those that He calls His children. He stands ready to fight for His children, and is ready to give them the instructions they need to fight and prevail against all who come against them.

Referring back to the Native Americans, the conduct of their styles of warfare is done in the natural and supernatural together. Before going into battle, Native American tribes would often sing songs of warfare. Two tribes that had powerful songs were the Apache and Comanche. When these tribes would sing their songs of war, their voices were often cries to wake the stirring spirit of each warrior preparing to do battle. Drums would be played, flutes would be blown, and the warriors and chiefs would shout to bring forth their warrior spirit. They would enter into battle afterwards with a spirit that had no fear and was ready to face any opposition that stood before them. This is among the many reasons that Native Americans had earned the title of braves.

When we conduct our songs of praise, and worship, we should be ready to bring about an atmosphere of war when needed. II Corinthians 10:3-5 tells us, *"For though we walk in the flesh, we are not waging war according to the flesh. For the weapons of our warfare are not of the flesh but have divine power to destroy strongholds. We destroy arguments and every lofty opinion that is raised against the knowledge of God, and take every thought captive to obey Christ."* What we manifest in the spirit can destroy the strongholds of the enemy.

Our knowledge of God and our power given by Him is the mightiest weapon of all. For that we must submit ourselves before God not only in humble adoration, but also to be instruments of war. As an archangel, Lucifer was also a warring angel. Like King David, Lucifer was a poet, musician, warrior, and soldier. He knows warfare, and how to wage war against his enemies. He is always ready to manipulate, destroy, and kill the servants of God who stand against him. I Peter 5:8 tells us about him, *"Be sober-minded; be watchful. Your adversary, the devil, prowls around like a roaring lion, seeking someone to devour."*

When David was a shepherd, lions and bears came to attack his flock. David once told of how a lion came and took a lamb from the flock. David immediately hunted the lion down and killed it. He did not have any bladed weapon like a sword or knife, but only a staff and a sling. Yet, David faced down the king of beasts, killed it, and took back the lamb that was about to be slain.

Like David, we too must be willing to fight against the enemy that seeks to take from us. We must become lions of the Lion of Judah. We must bear our fangs at the enemy, show the enemy we are the children of God, and devour them before they even get close to us. David killed the lion then took back the lamb. Jesus became the lamb that defeated the enemy that is Satan. We are to be like David and Jesus, willing to stand and fight all the strongholds of the wicked one.

Chapter Nine

Strongholds of the Wicked One, Enemies of the Spirit

The supernatural is full of enemies. Satan and his demons are just some of many different foes that come against the people of God. Warfare in the spirit is vast and dangerous. When making war, when singing songs and praises, there is always an enemy that is affected. The enemy that is targeted depends on who the cries of war from the believer are aimed. To know the enemy is to be one step ahead in battle. To know what we face also ensures our victory so God can then prepare us with His principles of war which are applied throughout the heavenly host.

As with all enemies in the natural realm, the enemies in the supernatural realm have several different classifications. These enemies have titles, ranks, soldiers, strongholds, dwelling places, and other positions including ones that could be described as terrorists and anarchist forces. These forces of the wicked one are vast, and have been around ever since the fall of Lucifer and his angels. While not an exact known number, we can estimate that one-third of the angelic host of heaven that fell with Lucifer was a large portion of the population of heaven. These forces could very well be in the millions, maybe even in the billions as we do not know just how vast the angelic host of God is.

These forces can often create strongholds of the wicked one. A stronghold by definition is a construction or building designed for the defense of territories in warfare, and to solidify rule in a region. The word stronghold (also called a fortification) is derived from the Latin words fortis, which means strong, and facere which means to make. Put together they then translate into the definition to make strong.

Jeremiah 33:22 confirms this stating, *"As the host of heaven cannot be numbered and the sands of the sea cannot be measured . . ."* This part of the scripture is similar to the description that God gave to Abraham in the book of Genesis in regards to the human population that would descend from him. To Abraham God also added another part to His prophecy. In Genesis 22:17 God said to Abraham, *"I will surely bless you, and I will surely multiply your offspring as the stars of heaven and as the sand that is on the seashore. And your offspring shall possess the gate of his enemies."* God's human creation would become vast just as the host of heaven, and we would possess the gates of our enemies. With God, we can bind our enemies that come against us in any form. We can take possession of them because we fight in the name of Jesus, who has dominion over all the forces of the wicked one as they bow before Him as the evil spirits of possessed people did when He walked the earth as man.

Just because we have possession of the enemy does not mean we should be ignorant of them. Our enemies are the enemies of God, and they hate all that is of God. Just like Satan, they seek to steal, kill, and destroy. Even people that don't believe in God are subject to these attacks of the dark ones who they are creations made in the image of God. All humanity is a reflection and an image of Jehovah. That makes all of humanity a target for the wicked ones that would come against us.

There are forces of demonic and worldly natures that we face. We must understand that when the angelic host that sided with Lucifer fell, the amount of forces that would become demons and fallen angels was vast. Their abilities and strengths varied. Their reigns and roles on the earth were unique according to each and every dark force that fell from the heavenly realm.

The book of Genesis tells us some things that occurred during the beginnings of man's real interactions with fallen angels. In Genesis 6:1-5, God tells us that the sons of God were attracted to the women of the earth. They interacted with these women by taking them as wives and having sexual relations with them. This led to the existence of giants and other individuals that were of angelic and human hybrids being birthed into the earth. This interbreeding of the creations of God also would give rise to the change in man's aging process such as instead of living into the 900 to 1,000 years range, man would be limited to only 120 years.

This mixing also caused God to see that these angels and their offspring were wicked with nothing but evil in their hearts and thoughts. Matthew 22:30 reads, *"For in the resurrection they neither marry nor are given in marriage, but are like the angels in heaven."* Angels don't marry, but there were certain fallen angels who chose to go against God's instructions and take wives and have offspring. This is the first understanding of what is inside the thoughts of the fallen sons of God, and just what their actions and intents were.

Jude 1:6 states, *"And the angels who did not stay within their own position of authority, but left their proper dwelling, he has kept in eternal chains under gloomy darkness until the judgment of the great day."* This scripture says that angels who were created for a specific purpose at one time had since abandoned their selected duty and chose to lead a corrupted nature from original purpose. They chose to embrace a negative existence opposite to a life of obedience to the God that created them.

We must see that all things have a free will. God created and designed all life to have a flow of free will and free nature to it. Angels are children of God as it says in Genesis when referring to them as "sons of God." As human beings, so do angels have free will, and more importantly, freedom of choice!

Satan was the first angel to ever choose to rebel against God, against his nature. He chose to rebel against his own position of power within God and His kingdom. His desire to be different from God and above Him resulted in

Lucifer being cast down to the earth and into the pit of hell. It is not known how the angels under Lucifer came to rebel against God. Perhaps Lucifer promised riches and glory if they sided with him. They may have gotten tired of obeying the will of God. They might have simply had an undying loyalty to the archangel who was over them. Whatever the reason for their rebellion, one-third of the heavenly host chose to side with Lucifer and attempt a coup de tat against God and His kingdom. In the end, they were stripped of what they once were and cursed to a negative and perverted existence in sin.

These forces are enemies that always are on the prowl. They are exactly like Satan in which they want to do nothing but to seek and destroy. Though their goal is the same, their methods and abilities are as different as they are vast. Each demonic or spiritual presence has unique strengths and powers. They can range from strong demonic forces that manifest over nations and cities to small spirits that spread negative influence over people. Knowing this truth is the beginning to understanding how to fight the advances of the wicked ones. When we realize their levels of strength, then we can then strategize using what God's principles of war to fight the attacks of the enemy.

There are several different classifications of enemies. Each different force could be an individual entity, a host of enemies working together, or an entire legion of a demonic presence that has manifested. Some spirits and demons have individual strengths that are so great they could control a nation by themselves. Legions of demons or spirits could be manifested often in several different places including, but not limited to, in a single individual. This kind of possession is so intense that it can cause a person possessed to act insane and become mentally unbalanced. These types of dark forces can manifest on supernatural and natural plains. These negative forces work through the mind, will, and emotions of a person's soul and can control them through the open door of a rebellious mind.

The supernatural nature of a demonic force can often be fed by the natural realm depending on what presence is being manifested and fed. A city that has a stronghold of the enemy present is often manifested and kept in strength by the generating of the negative things that feed it. An example of this can be seen in the city of San Francisco.

San Francisco had the first satanic church in its city limits. The church attracted over ten thousand followers to it and gradually increased in numbers. The founder of the church, Anton LaVey, published over 250,000 volumes of the satanic bible. He spread them all over the markets of San Francisco. Eventually, the church moved to Boulder, Colorado. We can assume though that the damage from the church was already done in the city of San Francisco. I believe many strongholds that were set in place then still have dominion over the city.

This example from San Francisco is just one example of what kind of problems can manifest within a city and can invite horrible spirits and demonic presences to establish themselves in cities. Such a widespread manifestation can also cause a difficult battle in the spirit for the forces of God. Though we have dominion over the enemy that does not mean that it is a walk in the park to get rid of them, or bring them down.

There are things that we need to begin to understand about these types of forces. We need to understand why praise and worship is vital in warfare against them. Atmospheres are generated from the influence of the world around them. Positive and negative forces can turn the air around us into a charged atmosphere of whatever it is that we produce.

Like the satanic church in San Francisco, a large majority of people that believe and practice things of an ungodly nature can turn a city or nation into a place devoid of God. We can see this from the example given in the story of the rich man and poor man in Luke 16:19-31. The rich man had all the money and power while the poor man had none and begged for food. The rich man died and went to hades (hell), while the poor man went to Abraham's bosom (a waiting room for the souls that would gain admittance into heaven by the death of Jesus on the cross}. The rich man asked if Lazarus could bring him a drink and cool his tongue. The answer was no.

God does not dwell in places that are devoid of Him. More specifically, God does not dwell in places devoid of His spirit. Hell and the lake of fire are places that are stored up for Satan and his angels. They are places that contain all the negative energies that come from man and Satan that do not accept the positive flowing of God and His Word. Ecclesiastes 9:5 tells us, *"For the living know that they will die, but the dead know nothing, and they have no more reward, for the memory of them is forgotten."*

God is a living constant positive while sin is a constant flowing of death and negative. All things that turn to God can become positive and flow in His living power. Sin however is a constant negative which never turns positive and never offers anything other than its constant conforming image. Because of this, God can't allow anything that has continued to walk in the flow of the negative of sin to enter into His dwelling place. That is the real purpose of hell and the lake of fire. To contain all the negativity of sin found in those that choose to operate in it.

The scripture that comes with warfare intelligence pertaining to the forces we fight against are in Ephesians 6:12. It states, *"For we do not wrestle against flesh and blood, but against the rulers, against the authorities, against the cosmic powers over this present darkness, against the spiritual forces of evil in the heavenly places."* These are the forces of the enemy that we face. These spiritual manifestations are numerous, and at times, very strong. These forces have their own strongholds that take root when given enough power.

Among these are those forces that manifest with the different emotional and mental problems that human beings face. These include depression, rebellion, rejection, hatred, fear, confusion, covetousness, nervousness, perversion, and many other negative spirits that manifest in humanity. (These strongholds are their own individual spirits.) They must be watched carefully for they can become strongholds at any time should they gain enough strength. Humanity gives these evil forces their strength by operating in fear, anxiety, worry, etc. When we don't take the negative thoughts captive they become stronger and stronger. Individually, they are dangerous enough for they attack all the things that are good of believers and non believers alike. No person is different in the attacks of the devil. All he cares about is destroying anyone that has God's image, namely humanity!

Our attitudes are often the first thing that can open the door to a negative influence. An example of this is pride. It's the state of being in a person that can make the attitude of a person become the downfall of the individual. Pride can become a spirit if not dealt with and taken authority over within a person's thinking. In Proverbs 16:18 we see that, *"Pride goes before destruction, and a haughty spirit before a fall."* We must to not give into pride. When we do, we release arrogance and then open ourselves up to things such as self-righteousness and vanity. This could lead a person down a road of destruction and ultimately a terrible fall!

Lucifer was the first person to be filled with pride. His pride led him to be cast out of heaven, stripped of all that he was, and have his gifts given to humans that he now despises and seeks to destroy. King Saul's pride gave rise to a huge ego that ultimately led him to lose his kingdom, his sanity, and his life. King Nebuchadnezzar of Babylon and the Chaldean Empire had several prideful moments in his life causing him to lose his position and ultimately his mind also.

Time and again he was warned by the prophet Daniel to beware of his pride. One day, Nebuchadnezzar got so prideful that he lost his sanity and ended up living like a wild animal in the wilderness in a house made of dung (possibly of both human and animal waste). All of these individuals who had such powers and authorities lost or taken away was because they let themselves be ruled by their pride.

The spirit of pride is manifested in the flesh. In order to operate in the spirit we must first crucify our flesh. To kill our flesh is to stop these negative spirits from manifesting. I say everyday that I rebuke my flesh; I embrace the spirit of God; Lord, cover me with the blood of Jesus and protect me from the attacks of the wicked one. It is in Jesus' blood that we are the most protected. The precious blood of Jesus is the one true protection that we have against the attacks of the enemy.

When we plead the blood over ourselves, our loved ones, and our dwelling places, we are giving ourselves a shield that can never be penetrated. His blood is full of life and power. Both are living, and bring about the positive flow of God that no negative force can operate or penetrate.

The book of Hebrews gives us testimony to how powerful Jesus' blood is due to the man that it belonged. Two scriptures from Hebrews give testimony to Jesus' endurance from hostility, and resistance to suffering due to temptation and other attacks. In Hebrews 2:18 we read, *"For because He Himself has suffered when tempted, He is able to help those who are being tempted."* Then, we read in Hebrews 12:3; *"Consider Him who endured from sinners such hostility against Himself, so that you may not grow weary or fainthearted."* Jesus lived life as a man and fought against all that we fight against in the flesh. This gave Him testimony to give His followers for experience to resist the attacks of the enemy, to put down our flesh, and to operate in what God gives us to fight off those attacks from our flesh. Jesus lived what He preached and walked in the same shoes all humans walk in to let us know He understands all that we go through. He did it in order to better relate to His creation, and to teach us how to walk in victory as humans. He did it and so can we through His blood, authority, and His name!

The second most effective tool after the blood is the praise and worship of the believer. Praise and worship will lead the believer to victory. It changes the atmosphere around the believer to create a positive and charged realm God to operate. This is where we make our own stronghold to stand against the strongholds of the wicked one.

Just as our enemy attacks us with many weapons, so does God give His creation their own weapons to attack and destroy! II Corinthians 10:4 says, *"For the weapons of our warfare are not of the flesh but have divine power to destroy strongholds."* God has created in us the same abilities that are in Him. This is something that all believers need to know. We are made in the image of God. The book of Genesis says that man is like God in knowledge, wisdom, and abilities. This means that God's divine power is capable of being wielded by His human creation. Our voices can be a divine weapon when used effectively. As an archangel, Lucifer was a warring angel as well as the chief worshiper. His gifts that God gave to us allow us to operate in this same authority. We can make war in the heavens with our voices and break down strongholds.

When a stronghold builds up in an area such as a neighborhood or community, it may then influence a whole city. A type of dome covering the whole of a city can build up from a stronghold. This dome can be the negative and demonic stronghold that establishes itself within the city. When the children of God began to fight against the stronghold, the man described seeing the dome pulling down and disappearing as it weakened. When the people of God stopped or slowed their attacks, then the dome grew back up over the city.

Strongholds dissipate when God's people pray, but a demonic stronghold will not be destroyed if the prayers stop. It's not enough to simply pray and go to church once in awhile. The believer must be willing to wage war against the enemy as many times as needed and for as long as it takes to get the victory.

When people know there is a demonic presence that must be defeated, then, the people must begin declaring war against it. The believer must pray, quote scripture, and, meditate on the words given by God. They must sing praise and worship to God to manifest the presence of the Holy Spirit to come and produce the changing atmosphere of healing and restoration. They must speak in agreement with other believers to build up the positive flow of God in those around them, and speak the word over their family and loved ones for protection. The believer must build up their faith and understanding in God so when they speak against evil, God will begin to operate through the power released through sound!. They must also be willing to have patience for a fight could take time. They must have endurance for any and all things that will come against them. They must have faith that all things will work together according to how God determines the outcome in accordance to what we ask of Him.

Often times when we face the enemy, either we will face it with others or alone. Do not get discouraged if you find yourself fighting against the enemy on your own. One soul with God can be a majority with Him. By grace we are saved in God, and our salvation is a weapon of God that is multiplied in abundance. II Peter 1:2 reads, *"May grace and peace be multiplied to you in the knowledge of God and of Jesus our Lord."* What we receive in Christ is multiplied by Him to advance our knowledge and understanding in Him.

Strongholds can have many methods of attack against whole populations. The spirits manifested from negative emotions can manifest in individuals that have several different reactions. These reactions are not only a negative atmosphere of demonic activity, but can also cause problems that affect the body physically.

Being in a world balanced between God, all good, and sin, all evil, the human body is influenced by positive and negative. What comes from the spiritual realm can either be of God or sin. The body when in interaction with these spiritual influences will take into it whatever it allows. Though we have to crucify our flesh daily as Paul told us, it is still our flesh. Our flesh does not control us, but we can be influenced by it. That can lead us to invite bad things into ourselves if we are not careful. This can lead to several outcomes that often will affect our health physically and mentally. Our spirit can then possibly affect others such as our family and friends.

The impact on family can be three things. The first is the individuals of the family can be influenced and impacted by what is manifested by someone affected from demonic or negative spirits. The second is that what affects the body can manifest and be passed to our offspring. This is a generational curse that will manifest in a child and can become the driving force in their lives. This is proven in the 34th chapter of the book of Exodus when God makes known that what comes from the father of a child will be passed onto a child. This gives rise to the third consequence. Sin nature, without repentance can be passed from one parent to child could become generational, affecting third, and fourth generations.

We read in Exodus 34:7, *"Keeping steadfast love for thousands, forgiving iniquity and transgressions and sin, but who will by no means clear the guilty, thus visiting the iniquity of the fathers on to the children and the children's children, to the third and the fourth generation."* God had come to the people of Israel and made known that while forgiveness is available those of a guilty or sinful nature, without repentance, have the possibility of passing their transgressions on to their descendents. This is where the term 'like father like son' comes to mind. It is not just a father that passes problems onto their kids, but mothers as well. Both parents have the potential to cause harm to their families, and both must be held accountable for their actions. This is why it is important to raise children carefully and correctly.

Hereditary traits are brought about by the transference of a parents DNA into their offspring. The traits of the parent are passed to their children from their blood. Like Christ's blood, our human blood has several unique qualities. Among them though can be the passing of generational curses. Not every person with a parent who has a sinful problem will inherit their parent's problems directly, but there is a possibility they can be influenced by what affected their parents. The body of a man or woman is open to the affects of the spirit and soul realms. The power of suggestion is often the beginning step to what comes over a person.

In athletics there is a study that has been developed to teach people how to listen to the body. The study focuses on the status of the central nervous system and its reactions to the body during training or exercise. While the interaction of the central nervous system and the body varies from individual to individual, what is agreed on is that the central nervous system, which controls emotion and emotional state, talks to the person stimulating it.

One result from observing the central nervous systems' communicating with its host is that if the person pays careful attention to what it is saying (or feeling what it wants them to feel), then the person who is training can change how they approach training dramatically. By listening to what the body is telling them, an athlete could remove stress or laziness as they begin to change their workout routine and what areas they need to improve or rest for better efficiency of performance and health. If neglected, then the body will still remain in the same condition or face worsening conditions such as injury or health problems.

The influence of the spirit on the body is the same way. Our emotions can trigger a spiritual response that can be good or bad for us. Our spirit and physical body are one. I Corinthians 15:44 makes this clear declaring, *"It is sown a natural body; it is raised a spiritual body."* If there is a natural body, then there is also a spiritual body. We have to be aware of both. We need to listen to them and be aware of what we put into them. This means we have to approach with caution and discernment when we listen. II Corinthians 7:1 tells us, *"Since we have these promises, beloved, let us cleanse ourselves from every defilement of body and spirit, bringing holiness to completion in the fear of God."* Our warfare begins and ends with our bodies and our souls.

One good method of stopping strongholds from being formed is to listen carefully to what we allow into our spirit and body. To stop something from ever taking root begins with our listening. God expects us to listen to Him as believers, but also expects us to use our wisdom and knowledge to make good decisions in our daily lives. He wants us to be strong in our thinking and use His teachings to build ourselves up to know immediately what He would do for us. A father will teach his children, and children will learn what they are taught. God as Father teaches His children and expects His children to learn and apply what He teaches. This is called using Godly wisdom and knowledge.

Every person in the world is what God and Satan wage war over. The soul of man is the most precious thing to both. For God, it is His precious creation that He loves and wants to be in relationship. For Satan, we are the instruments he can use to hurt God. For every soul he steals from God is a victory for Satan.

I believe that Satan is firmly aware of what awaits him when Jesus returns and establishes His kingdom. His moment in the Lake of Fire is burned into his mind making Satan realize his imminent fate. The one thing that will give Satan any kind of real victory lies in the souls that end up in hell with him. For this he will stop at nothing to destroy the creation that Jesus paid the price. This is what makes Satan relentless in his attacks against us.

Aside from the tools of listening and discernment, God has given us a weapon that once belonged to the devil. Our praise and worship once was the gift that Lucifer possessed when he was the chief worshiper of God. After his fall Lucifer was stripped of his abilities in music, sound, praise and worship. All these gifts were given to us by God for every individual that was made in His image. God gave us the ability to use the powerful and anointed gifts of Lucifer against him for the glory of God. Our praise and worship is a powerful weapon against the enemy. It can devastate and utterly destroy them when it becomes powerful enough.

The cries of praise and worship are powerful agents of warfare. What we ring out in the natural realm is a wall of fire in the supernatural realm. Positive voices and emotions of desire for God are instruments that manifest strongly in the atmosphere. This creates the presence of God that has dominion over all demonic and negative forces. The thing to understand though is that when using praise and worship in warfare, it is not just a one shot solution. In areas that have strongholds built the manifesting of God's presence with praise and worship must be an ever flowing constant.

Enemy forces can leave for a time and then come back. Throughout human history, militaries have often fought again and again over positions of strategic value and importance in certain regions throughout the world. These places of fortitude had tremendous strategic advantage, and it was for this reason that militaries would fight to capture or recapture them.

Places that can have an outpouring of God's presence can weaken overtime. If we are not constantly building up our spiritual strength, then we are losing ground. This weakening gives the enemy the advantage to sneak in and take over, sometimes. We see this all throughout ancient Israel where the people of God would turn from Him, be taken over, go back to God, and reclaim their territory only to have the same results repeated multiple times. This was the reason that God had so many different prophets and judges spread throughout the history of the Old Testament. Because the people turned from Him, God would then send people to speak so to make the people listen and repent, or more bad things would happen to them because of their disbelief, and lack of spiritual discipline until they wised up and turned back to God.

Another type of enemy force that is powerful are principalities. A principality by definition is a sovereign state ruled over by an individual with a prince or princedom title. Several times throughout the Bible there are mentions of nations with spiritual principalities. After the classes of enemy forces listed in Ephesians 6:12, you can easily see a principality when you read the book of Daniel!

The book of Daniel is filled with several stories of supernatural forces and warfare. Daniel was a man of great anointing from God. One of his talents was that of prophecy concerning future events. One story that is mentioned about Daniel's visions of the future is seen in the 10th chapter.

During Daniels captivity in Babylon (located in modern day Iraq) under the reign of Cyrus of Persia, Daniel received a word from the Lord. While Daniel understood what the vision was, he did not fully grasp what it meant.

He was in great conflict for this reason and sought answers from God for over twenty-one days.

For twenty-one days Daniel received no answer from God, and it greatly troubled him. We can assume that Daniel had bouts of great stress and possibly depression over this as His voice of knowledge and wisdom was silent for a great length of time. Finally, on the twenty-fourth day of the month, the archangel Gabriel came to Daniel to give him instruction from God.

Gabriel informed Daniel that God had heard his prayers for understanding and had responded immediately to them. The problem that had caused God's replies to be delayed had to do with Gabriel's battle with a being referred to as the prince of Persia. In Daniel 10:13, Gabriel tells Daniel that, *"The prince of the kingdom of Persia withstood me twenty-one days, but Michael, one of the chief princes, came to help me, for I was left there with the kings of Persia."* From this scripture, we can assess many things about enemy principalities.

First, they are like the angelic forces of heaven in which, like Michael and Gabriel, they are what we would consider the elite or special forces of the heavenly host. Second, these princes are appointed over nations and empires of the world. Third, they are extremely strong enemies. So strong in fact that they can stop or delay God's work from getting done. This is made evident in the fact that it took two archangels just to get through to Daniel with the word God had for him. The fourth and final revelation we can gather from this scripture is that not only are there princes, but kings of the enemy. It is not fully understood what this title of 'kings of Persia' means. What is to be known is that they are present in the nations.

We read further in the chapter that after Daniel had been comforted and had his strength returned after his ordeal of conflict and suffering over his visions from God, Gabriel told Daniel that he was going back to fight against the prince of Persia, and also against the prince of Greece. This is told in Daniel 10:20, *"Soon I must return to fight against the spirit prince of the kingdom of Persia, and then against the spirit prince of the kingdom of Greece."* This scripture reveals that not only are there more princes, but also the term 'spirit prince' is used to describe them. Further reading in verse 10:21 has Gabriel telling Daniel, *"Before I do that, I will tell you what is written in the Book of Truth. There is no one to help me against these spirit princes except Michael, your spirit prince I have been standing beside Michael as his support and defense since the first year of the reign of Darius the Mede."*

This leads to a theory that there are earthly princes of God that have authority over certain nations. While speculative, we could surmise that certain nations with a declaration of loyalty to God are among these kinds of nations. Nations such as the United States of America (one nation under God), the nation Israel (with Michael being its chief prince and protector), the African nation of Ethiopia (who descend from Abraham and have sworn to defend Israel in times of war), the African nation of Zambia (where former president Frederick Chiluba decreed Zambia a Christian nation), and many others have a presence and submission to the Lord God.

There are nations that have given themselves over to the Lordship of Jesus Christ. While some nations do waver or sometimes fall short of the Glory of God, they are still nations that have a spirit of God in them. This then could establish godly princes over them to guard, guide, direct, and protect them at all times of obedience and service (something I declare in my prayers every night over my family and friends). If God gives us guardian angels for our own individual protection, then it is very possible He appoints these same kinds of angels over nations and cities as well. This is made evident in Psalm 91:11-16:

"For He will order His angels to protect you wherever you go.
They will hold you with their hands to keep you from striking your foot on a stone.
You will trample down lions and poisonous snakes; you will crush fierce lions and serpents under your feet!
The Lord says, "I will rescue those who love me. I will protect those who trust in my name.
When they call on me, I will answer; I will be with them in trouble.
I will rescue them and honor them.
I will satisfy them with long life and give them my salvation."

Gabriel stated to Daniel that he often had to fight the other princes alone, and only had Michael as backup when needed. This is possibly due to the fact that while there are princes of God, there are not many appointed to wage war on the same level as these two archangels. All angels are created with a unique purpose and function designated to them by God. The ones that did not fall or twist their nature to something perverted or evil are worthy and loyal servants to God. Like man, they have to wage war against the forces of the wicked one sometimes through very hard circumstances and trials. Anyone who chooses God over the world will always face uphill battles. This is made evident for angels as they face enemies that can be both strong principalities and strongholds.

An enemy presence that is made into a stronghold or principality can be fed the same way that praise and worship feeds the atmosphere of God. All flowing of things positive and negative have an interaction with individual things and places. People can produce the same positive and negative aspects from their own thoughts and voices. This could be described as a source of energy for negative and demonic spirits as well as a positive energy for God. All of this depends on the manner in which we choose to feed the atmosphere that we are creating. Are we creating an atmosphere for God to move, or an atmosphere for a stronghold of the enemy to manifest?

Scientist and engineering genius Nikola Tesla was a man devoted to the harnessing and distributing of energy. Unlike Thomas Edison, who created the telephone via wires and cables, Tesla had found a way to send signals and electricity through the air without wires or any matter based object long before the technology for such science even existed. Cell phones and radios today would not be as they are had it not been for Tesla and his discoveries.

Tesla was brilliant when it came to studying the interactions of atmosphere and electricity. He understood that the earth itself was in constant rotation and vibration to maintain a constant charge of electrical energy to keep it moving and operating as a place where life could flourish. He understood the earth to be an electrically charged body.

Tesla once said, "The earth was found to be, literally, alive with electrical vibrations," when describing what he saw in the earth. Tesla said that the planet earth was like a conductor of limited dimensions, and that whatever was transmitted into the atmosphere was where unlimited power could be manifested depending on what source of energy was being used. Tesla described the human voice as a source of energy to transmit power that was unlimited, for the human voice never ended as it was used not by one person, but all of humanity. Tesla knew that whatever was put into the atmosphere could affect the area it resided over.

Hearing is based on what is spoken or heard by a person. The words heard are transmitted through the air and into a person's ear. In the spirit, words can be heard by the mind, heart, and ear. The spirit tells us things that are often not heard by others, and yet we can describe some of what is spoken as actual words that we hear.

What we speak or give worship to often has consequences based on positive and negative manifestations from words spoken. The book of Revelation has two scriptures that give examples of what is produced from a positive and a negative spoken word. For the positive, we read in Revelation 2:7, *"He who has an ear, let him hear what the spirit says to the churches. To the one who conquers I will grant to eat of the tree of life, which is in the paradise of God."* The results of listening to things positive from God give us the paradise of God. For the negative, Revelation 14:11 says, *"And the smoke of their torment goes up forever and ever, and they have no rest, day or night, these worshipers of the beast and its image, and whoever receives the mark of its name."* Those that chose to follow down a negative path, and who listen to negative things of the spirit have consequences of nothing but pain and suffering.

While the book of Revelation is prophetic, the scriptures tell us what happens when we choose God or the ways of the devil. An atmosphere based on negative things can open the doors for sin to enter. Sin is what feeds the demonic enemies and makes them strong. It was the nature of sin in Persia and Greece that caused powerful princes to rise up and reside over them.

These nations had given into practices ranging from worship of false gods and pagan images to perverse ways of living. This produced a profane atmosphere that allowed all sorts of spirits to enter and manifest. From this atmosphere we see in history that these great nations of Greece and Persia would later be given over to Roman and Arab Empires, become divided, have their identities taken away, made to conform to their conquerors cultural images, and finally pass away never to rise again.

Negative atmospheres will often produce spirits of chaos, confusion, and division. Throughout modern history, a good example of this kind of atmosphere could be revealed in the Muslim world. The Islamic religion has different denominations that have very strict views of each other. Sunni, Shiite, and Sufi religious practices often give rise to certain views of prejudice against each other based on what they perceive as the correct way of worshiping and following their god (Allah). As a unified voice that worships together five times every day, it could be agreed that their worship is feeding a spirit that manifests in each person. This then produces a spirit that causes other negative emotions to stir. This could be why many Muslim views today are of a hateful nature towards others.

The way the Middle East is today makes this apparent. The Arab Spring, which is the revolt of the Arab people in their respected nations such as Libya, Tunisia, Egypt, and Syria against their governments, in the Middle East produced civil wars, government collapses, and all out death and anarchy. What is even harder to realize is that the spirits produced from these Arab Springs seem to have no end to them. In countries like Egypt and Syria, the populations of both countries seem to have no control over the people or each other.

Every time a new government is made, or whenever two opposing forces seem to have reached a point of negotiation for peaceful solutions, then the people find a problem with the new government or another faction rises up and commits revolution. Whatever is the reason behind these Arab Springs, chaos, division, and strife seem to have no end in these countries. All the fighting seems to simply begin again and again over and over.

The enemies of God can be fed the same way that the spirit of God is fed. Praise and worship is used in many other religions throughout the world. While not all religions are about spreading negativity or worshiping bad things, different religious practices do have false ideologies and pagan images that people worship. Giving your faith and belief in these things will lead you down a bad path. It is for this reason that you have to tread cautiously wherever you go.

You must be aware of what you are getting yourself into, listening to, or with whom you are associating. God knows that not every person in the world believes or will believe in Him. That doesn't mean that He wants people to believe in false things. In terms of people that speak, God warns in Matthew 7:15, *"Beware of false prophets, who come to you in sheep's clothing but inwardly are ravenous wolves."* In listening to those who speak on things from the spirit, God gives a warning. In I John 4:1 He warns, *"Beloved, do not believe every spirit, but test the spirits to see whether they are from God, for many false prophets have gone out into the world."*

We have to be aware of the things that are taught to us on what is in the world. God expects us to use our brains when
discerning things. He wants us to think and to question things. False prophets, bad teachers, and negative people never change. 2 Timothy 3:13 states, *"Evil people and imposters go from bad to worse, deceiving and being deceived."* By giving into what these kinds of people tell us, then we basically have become the same kind of people.

As a creation made in God's image we have a responsibility to think on His level and know what we are doing. This is what will ultimately help us in knowing what it is we are getting ourselves into with regards to the spirit. Evil spirits can deceive people into thinking they are hearing from God. This is one way that strongholds and principalities can take dominant positions within us or society. We have to use discernment of knowledge and wisdom in order to be able to tread through the waters of what is good and what is evil.

Our enemy has the ability to use any and all means of warfare to their advantage to deal crushing blows to God. When we don't have a good understanding of what looks right or wrong this is where we must be held accountable. God will help us to defeat our enemy, but we have to be willing to open our own eyes to see the enemy or at least attempt to see them. This will help us to better walk with God for we are using our soul and spirit and seeing more clearly with God's help.

Psalm 119:105 gives good direction. *"Your word is a lamp to my feet and a light to my path."* God will guide us through His word, but it is our feet and path that we take. Our way to God is through salvation, but we all have a path in life that we each take. The end result for every true believer is eternity in heaven with God, but, we all still have a life to lead here on earth.

We must be careful of the enemies of this world, never letting ourselves become vulnerable to them. We have to be willing to listen to the voice of God, to build up an atmosphere with Him through praise and worship, knowledge and wisdom, understanding and discernment. If we want to keep strongholds and principalities from manifesting in our dwelling places, then it is up to us to stand and wage war against them from ever being made.

God makes mighty men and women for battle. He gives us all sorts of tools to wage war against our enemy to destroy them. If we follow His word, use praise and worship to build up the atmosphere, speak to the enemy and deny them their domain, in Jesus' name, then we can cast out all demons and negativity that comes against us.

This is how we can build up ourselves, our cities, and our nations to become godly places of dwelling.

Romans 4:17 states, *"As it is written 'I have made you the father of many nations' in the presence of God in whom he believed, who gives life to the dead and calls into existence the things that do not exist."* When we take instruction from God, then we can build up places that are invincible. We can make that which is godly and mighty. We can make a constant place of positive atmosphere that no enemy can come against. That is a godly domain and dwelling place.

Chapter Ten

Conviction, Heart
Change, and Salvation

What would we consider the most important part of praise and worship? What is it that is brought about during the time of praise and worship that is the best of all of the wonders that come from this time of devotion to God? While all that is produced from praise and worship is nothing short of wondrous, what we could say is most vital is when someone comes to the Father.

The atmosphere produced through praise and worship is so many things. It is an atmosphere of change, of healing, of manifesting the Holy Spirit, and the moving of the Father through His children. What is also brought about is the moment when someone feels the coming of the conviction of the heart. That time when a person will seek salvation and become a new creature in Christ Jesus.

What is salvation? What does that word really mean when we think about it in league with the Creator of all life? Let's take a moment to go into some details about just what salvation really is. Salvation is the start to restoration in God.

How does salvation lead to restoration? The Word says in Acts 3:21, *"Whom heaven must receive until the time for restoring all the things about which God spoke by the mouth of His holy prophets long ago."* The prophets of the Old Testament foretold of the time when Jesus would come to the earth, die, and save us from sin. In doing this, Jesus then gave us new life and a completion to become what we were meant to be with Him. Romans 6:23 says, *"For the wages of sin is death, but the free gift of God is eternal life in Christ Jesus our Lord."*

Jesus is often seen as the last Adam. The first Adam and Jesus are compared in I Corinthians 15:22, *"For as in Adam all die, so also in Christ shall all be made alive."* Adam was the first man ever made. When he sinned he allowed death to enter into life and with it the condemnation of man to hell due to his sin. When Jesus came into the world by being born of an earthly mother but having God as His Father, He kept the covering of sin off Him. After dying as a man and a perfect creation not born into sin, Jesus completed a circle that started with Adam bringing new death but ending with Jesus bringing new life.

Jesus died not in sin like Adam, but with sin taken into Him to pay for all sin. I Peter 3:18 states, *"For Christ also suffered once for sins, the righteous for the unrighteous, that He might bring us to God, being put to death in the flesh but made alive in the spirit."* By dying in the flesh, Jesus then manifested new life in the spirit. He fulfilled all the prophecies that were to be fulfilled by Him, and showed His truth in doing so.

The truth of what Jesus spoke is seen in John 14:8, *"I am the way, the truth, and the life. No one comes to the Father except through me."* Jesus restored our relationship with Him through His death. As the last Adam, Jesus was the complete man who God had made originally before the fall. After Jesus, man now had access to this same completion in Christ. In order to become this complete man, we must begin with accepting the truth of how it came about for us.

Salvation leads to the desire and need to tell the truth. To tell the truth is to confess to God your willingness to believe in Him, and to believe Him. This means that you are accepting Him as God. Romans 10:9-10 says, *"Because, if you confess with your mouth that Jesus is Lord and believe in your heart that God raised Him from the dead, you will be saved. For with the heart one believes and is justified, and with the mouth one confesses and is saved."* Confessing brings about belief.

When people put their belief into something that is real, then it produces real results. It gives back to the belief that we put into it. We produce the ability to have stronger faith because we had the knowledge that it is not false, but true. When something is false and we put our faith and belief into it, then that will produce the return of deceit or hurt. That will cause us to lose faith and belief, and make us question whether putting belief into something else is going to lead us down the same road.

Jesus had every intention of making sure that what He was teaching us to have belief in was backed up with truth. He gave proof that it was real. He backed up everything He taught and showed everything to prove that He was real.

Jesus gave proof of His existence and the existence of God by becoming a man. As the last Adam, Jesus demonstrated the godly life that people could have in relationship with God. He showed how man could be so much more when they allowed the Holy Spirit to come and live inside of them. Jesus performed miracles, healed people, walked on water, and raised the dead back to life.

Jesus was not only on the earth to die for the sins of humanity. He was also present on the earth to show how a person could become complete in God when they accepted Him, who they were in Christ, and what a person could do when they allowed the Holy Spirit to come and live in them. Jesus was teaching humanity to be godly, act godly, and to live a godly life.

This great godly existence begins with confession. Confession between God and people can bring about change in a person's life. James 5:16 confirms this, *"Therefore confess your sins to one another and pray for one another, that you may be healed. The prayer of a righteous person has great power as it is working."*

Confession is telling the truth about something. Confessing is admittance. Confession in this manner can lead to things like courage, honesty, integrity, responsibility, and accountability. We all confess things to others for a variety of reasons. If we are responsible for our actions, then we are responsible for our own truths. This is what God wants from us in our confessions to Him. He wants our truth to be confessed to Him. He wants us to be held accountable to what we say to Him.

To approach God in the spirit with truth and confession is all God ever wants. To ask for forgiveness of sin is asking God to separate us from everyone else who stays in sin. I John 1:9 states, *"If we confess our sins, He is faithful and just to forgive us our sins and to cleanse us from all unrighteousness."*

Why do we ask for forgiveness, have we done something wrong? There is a fault of man that separates us from God. Adam and Eves mistakes in the Garden of Eden created a state of rebellion that is present in man today. This makes every person a rebel against God in their own way. It is for this reason that we must ask for forgiveness of our sins. We could look at forgiveness in God like this. As salvation leads to restoration, then forgiveness leads to separation from the conformed image that the rest of humanity embraces in sin.

Salvation, confession, and forgiveness are all it takes to become one with God. The thing to understand though is that no one really feels this until a certain moment in time. No one is born with a deep desire to submit to God or seek His love. We have to go through life waiting for that moment when we feel Him tugging at our hearts. People walk in a world that often blinds them to the ideas of a spiritual world, a living God, and a desire to be more than what they are. People have to be willing to pay attention to the things of God, to listen to friends and family who want to help them to meet God, and be willing to go to the places like church or meetings that have the presence of God in them.

God understands that some people require a period of growth to learn about Him, to understand Him, and to accept Him. In some cases this can actually be a great benefit because the person who is willing to learn about God will develop traits that they will require in their future walks with God. Traits such as patience, understanding, asking the right questions, and a need to learn are all attributes of a godly believer for they help a person become more like the Creator who made them in His image.

Praise and worship produces moments that make someone feel the need to come to God. It's not always about the message the pastor or minister speaks. Sometimes it is about the atmosphere that is manifested in which God can flow.

A person who comes to where there is real praise and worship going on and where people are flowing in the spirit can sometimes feel the presence of God in their midst. Their willing heart that they come to the place where worship is happening opens them up to the possibility of feeling Him. Not everyone who goes to church or ministry meetings come seeking God. Some go because they feel obligated to go to church, others to make people, like spouses or parents, happy, and a few because it gives them something to do. This is common practice in the world today.

A person that is seeking something from God, or a person who is willing to go and see if God is real or to really learn about Him and His message of salvation is a person who then is no longer tuned out to God. They legitimately come to God with interest in Him. Even the mildest of interest is something that God can use for His glory.

A little bit of interest in God is like a tiny measure of faith. God favors faith even in the smallest amounts. Matthew 17:20 tells us, *"He said to them, "Because of your little faith. For truly, I say to you, if you have faith like a grain of mustard seed, you will say to this mountain, 'Move from here to there,' and it will move, and nothing will be impossible for you."* A person willing to come and at least be there in church is giving into the idea of listening. This is called faith listening. Romans 10:17 reads, *"So faith comes from hearing, and hearing through the word of Christ."*

Praise and worship is hearing the word as music and sound from God. If the praise and worship is true, then it allows the movement of God and the Holy Spirit. That can create a feeling of God tugging at the person's heart. In the midst of the movement of God the heart that is seeking Him and putting their faith in Him opens up. God then puts a conviction into the person's heart to run to Him and ask for forgiveness. For this feeling of conviction for God though, the convicted heart must then be willing to change for God.

People can pray a prayer, hear the word of God, and can accept God in their heads as real and true. What makes a true believer though is not a head change, but a change of the heart. It is in the heart that the true temple of God is. It is in the heart of man that God wishes to reside. To accept God into your heart means you must be willing to change your heart and turn it to God. That is when God fully sees your commitment and obedience to Him.

The heart change is where the real change happens. Submitting to God willingly through salvation is what causes the heart to become complete in God. This change is where you realize just what you really have become as a new creature in Christ Jesus. The heart is the door to where the temple of God resides. When it turns to God, a change can be felt inside. Your whole being is different after you receive Jesus as Lord and Savior. You are still you, but now more complete than you ever were. You are forgiven and restoration has begun.

When salvation is accepted during praise and worship, there is a different flowing of the spirit. Unlike the alter calls that a pastor will give at the end of a church service, salvation in the spirit is felt through the flowing of the sounds of God. Music played to honor God, melody of instruments, and voices of song and prayer bring about a powerful atmosphere that creates holy ground.

Chapter Eleven

The Pursuit to Uncover God's Secrets

My whole life has been one of fascination with things that are different. Ever since I was a young boy, I have always sought to learn about all things unique. Being raised in ministry, I was introduced to so many different people, places, and areas of study and wonder.

You could say that I had a personality for exploring. One area of exploring I enjoyed was in the study of animals. I absolutely loved studying about animals when I was really young. At school during my early days in 2nd and 3rd grade, I was always reading the Zoo Books magazines that our classes had. I had never been so attached to anything else until I picked up my first Zoo Book magazine. When the school semester would end, I would go up to my teacher and ask her if I could keep the periodicals because they were my favorite things to read. Even when they had gotten outdated I still kept reading the ones I had taken home from school simply because I never got tired of what they said about animals.

Another place of study that I loved to read about and learn was that of different cultures. My father had been all over the world and I loved to hear about all the places that he had been in his travels. My favorite stories were the ones of when he went to the African nation of Zambia. To this day I still never get tired of hearing about all the things that he used to do in foreign countries, the people he met, or what he did for God over there. From his stories, I had developed a great love of different people and cultures that I still have to this day.

When it came to my studies of God, I was always interested in the stories from the Bible. My mother would read to me from books such as Christian Mother Goose and Christian story books when I was very little. When I got old enough to read on my own, I didn't read the Bible in the usual sense you might think of as a kid. When I read the word of God, I would read multiple different Bibles. My book shelf as a kid had a regular Bible, an illustrated Bible, a comic book Bible, and The Adventure Bible which taught me history and science from the Bible times. I could not get enough of them.

I must have driven my parents crazy as a kid asking them all sorts of questions about things I did not know or was curious. I loved reading the Word, and it was from this love that sparked my interest in further understanding of who God is, what the life He created was about, and all the other wonders of Him that I still fascinate over today.

After Gabrielle's passing, was when I began to take a different look at the world. I began to become fascinated with things such as the end times and other studies of the supernatural realm. I fell in love with learning about the end times. My first book I fully finished and studied in the Bible was the book of Revelation. There were other books of the Bible I read, but never studied as thoroughly as I did Revelation. Sometimes I was scared of what I read while other times I was in a state of wonder over them. I would read other books and watch TV shows that educated me on subjects like the tribulation, the anti-Christ, and the rapture.

I spent three to five years studying about the end times. This was all when I was about 13 to 17 years of age. When I had reached the climax of my studies, I then began to take an interest in other areas of study. I think it would be best to say that my studies of the end times opened me up to learning just about everything. I began to take a great love in history, science, mathematics, and writing.

As I entered into community college after high school, I was not really into the college classes I took. I passed everything, but was still not very interested in what the courses taught. I would often take other books with me to class to read and learn from while I simply took notes from the blackboards of the classes I took. Still, I was learning and growing in knowledge day in and out.

After graduating with a liberal arts degree from College of the Desert in Palm Desert, CA, I then entered into the university level of college education. After first trying for an English degree, I then changed to History after being accepted at Cal State San Bernardino. Before actually going to Cal State, I first went back to COD to earn two more degrees in history and anthropology. I also took to studying and majoring in philosophy and political science but never received degrees in them as I had already attained two social science degrees with history and anthropology, and two degrees was the maximum in the field of social science. Still, I admit that my time attaining these degrees was where my real expertise in science and history finally took hold of me.

While at Cal State, I had begun my work towards two bachelor's degrees in pastoral theology and biblical studies. Let me just say that going for three bachelor level degrees at the same time can be a handful! Still, all my hard work and dedication paid off and I earned three different bachelor level degrees in history, pastoral theology, and biblical studies.

The reason that I studied all these different areas was because of my love of learning. My love of God had opened me up to the desire to learn all I can about the great creations that He has made. Being made in the image of God, I feel I have a mind to learn, to create, and to establish myself on the levels that God has made for me.

I always believed that when you read and study the Bible, and try to understand them from a real life perspective that you can see that God gave us the Word to help make life better for us, more complete. Every person in the Bible faced real life problems that we all face today. All the things that we see go on in the world today like depression, stress, family problems, work problems, etc., are issues that everyone in the Bible went through. Each person had to learn to see things from Gods point of view. They had to be willing to give God's commandments an ounce of faith. They had to endure hardships, criticisms, and other problems that came with doings things God's way.

One of my greatest desires is to adapt all the things that we see in the Bible to what we all do today. I want to establish a way of thinking and acting that comes from application from the Word, by giving yourself over to God, and letting the Holy Spirit guide us. Living this way brings us to higher levels of excellence. When we give ourselves to God, and the Holy Spirit, then we become like the Last Adam. We become more like Jesus.

The study of praise and worship produces this kind of understanding. The knowledge that an atmosphere in which manifesting presence of God, where there is a flowing of the Holy Ghost, produces changes in people. Healing, restoration, closer intimacy with God, knowledge and understanding, and much more all come from a place of real praise and worship to God. My studies into other cultures have proven that there is indeed more to the use of praise and worship, and that there are millions of people and ways of praise and worship to God that not only please Him, but show true devotion to Him.

There is more to uncover, to study, and to understand from God. That drive makes me have a great desire to study all the mysteries of God's great creation, both in the natural, and the supernatural realms. Philippians 1:6 says, *"He who has begun a good work in you will complete it until the day of Jesus Christ."* Praise and worship can bring about the wonders of God. I hope to discover more of His great mysteries all the days of my life!

About the Author

Dr. Harry Assad Salem III is author of over ten books including children's literature and scholarly studies. He is a graduate of California State University San Bernardino, Newburgh Seminary and College of the Bible, and Heritage University and Seminary.

Dr. Salem holds five earned doctorates in archaeology, biblical studies, theology, religious education, and practical ministry. He also holds an honorary doctorate in divinity. Dr. Salem is the creator of the children's book series Learning Pals that he created to teach children about ethics and morals.

He has been an ordained minister with Salem Family Ministries for over ten years. Dr. Salem is also a world class strongman and champion powerlifter with several championships and titles. His motto is "Excellence is excellent," and makes the effort to live every day by a standard of excellence for success and prosperity.

Books by Dr. Harry Assad Salem III

Grave Raiders

Feminine Spirits & Angels

Age of Mystery

Investigating Wonders

Grave Raiders

Learning Pals Children's Series:

Count of Ten Say Amen *children's book*

Ten Steps to Build and be Spirit Filled *children's book*

Counting Ten Fingers for Patience *children's book*

Ten Shots for Do and Don't *children's book*

If you would like to read more of Dr. Salem's books you can find them online at the website www.salemfamilyministries.org. You can also find them at Amazon.com, Barnes&Noble.com, and Walmart.com under the name Dr. Harry Salem III.

To Contact **Harry Salem III**, write:

Salem Family Ministries
P. O. Box 1595
Cathedral City, CA 92235

For More Information about Harry Salem III
or Salem Family Ministries'
products please find our web site
www.salemfamilyministries.org
Salem Family Ministries YouTube Channel

Bibliography

Batterson, Mark. *Primal.* Colorado Springs, CO: Multnomah Books, 2010.

Indian Spirit. New York, NY: MJF Books, 2006.

Kent, David. *Tesla The Wizard of Electricity.* New York, NY: Fall River Press, 2013.

Salem, Cheryl, Salem, Harry. *An Angel's Touch.* Tulsa, OK: Harrison House, 1997.

Salem, Cheryl. *A Bright Shining Place.* Tulsa, OK: Eagle Run Publishing, 1981.

Salem, Cheryl. *Rebuilding The Ruins of Worship.* Tulsa, OK: Thomas Nelson Inc., 2012.

Oral Roberts Edition. *Holy Bible King James Version.* Tulsa, OK: Oral Roberts Evangelistic Association, Inc., 1981.

www.openbible.info/topics/esv (English Standard Version Bible).

Made in the USA
Columbia, SC
27 June 2023